W9-BVE-222

THEOLOGIANS TODAY: YVES M.-J. CONGAR, OP

Other titles in the THEOLOGIANS TODAY series:

Hans Urs von Balthasar
F. X. Durrwell, CSSR
Hans Küng
Henri de Lubac, SJ
Karl Rahner, SJ
Edward Schillebeeckx, OP
F. J. Sheed

THEOLOGIANS TODAY: a series selected and edited
by Martin Redfern

YVES M.-J. CONGAR, OP

SHEED AND WARD · LONDON AND NEW YORK

First published 1972

Sheed & Ward Inc, 64 University Place, New York, N.Y. 10003
and Sheed & Ward Ltd, 33 Maiden Lane, London WC2E 7LA

Nihil obstat: John M. T. Barton, S.T.D., L.S.S
Imprimatur: ✠ Victor Guazzelli, V.G.
Westminster, 15 May, 1972

Library of Congress Catalog Number 72-2167

This book is set in 12/14 Monotype Imprint

Made and printed in Great Britain by
Billing & Sons Limited, Guildford and London

CONTENTS

Introduction   7

1. Holy Spirit and Spirit of Freedom   9

2. Scripture Revelation, Church, and Tradition   47

3. Liturgy, Principal Instrument of the Church's
   Tradition   79

4. The Council as an Assembly and the Church
   as essentially Conciliar   101

49110

Sources and Acknowledgments

"Holy Spirit and Spirit of Freedom" (1959) is from *Laity, Church, and World*, London, Geoffrey Chapman, 1960; and New York, Helicon, 1960.

"Scripture, Revelation, Church, and Tradition" (1963) and "Liturgy, Principal Instrument of the Church's Tradition" (1963) are both from *Tradition and Traditions*, London, Burns & Oates, 1966 and Sheed & Ward, 1970; and New York, Macmillan, 1966.

"The Council as an Assembly and the Church as essentially Conciliar" (1964) is from *One, Holy, Catholic, and Apostolic*, ed. Herbert Vorgrimler, London, Sheed & Ward, 1968.

INTRODUCTION

The last twenty-five years, and in particular the last ten years, have seen a remarkable flowering of Roman Catholic theology. But for the non-specialist—for the busy parish priest, the active layman, the student—the very wealth of this development presents a range of problems. With which theologian does he begin? Which theologians will he find the most rewarding? Can he ignore any of them?

There are no quick or final answers to such questions, of course, but I hope that this new *Theologians Today* series will help many Catholics to find their own answers more easily. It is designed to achieve two main purposes. Each individual book provides a short but representative introduction to the thought of an outstanding Catholic theologian of the present day, and the series as a whole demonstrates the kind of relationship existing between the best contemporary Catholic theology and official Church teaching.

Both purposes are met by the framework common to all the books. For each book I have selected—and arranged in order of original publication—four pieces which indicate the range in time, approach, and special interest of the theologian concerned. Partly to make my selections more 'objective', but mainly to emphasize the close connection between the theologian's writing and the teaching of Vatican II, I have keyed the articles to the four major documents of that Council—the four Constitutions, on the Church, on Revelation, on the Liturgy, and on the Church in the Modern World.

The selections are very much my own. The theologians themselves, or other editors, would doubtless have made different choices. Nevertheless, I feel that—granted my self-imposed limitations of space and conciliar theme, and the further necessary limitations imposed by copyright or by a proper preference for the out-of-print or inaccessible over the widely available—I have dome my own best for men to whom I owe a large debt of gratitude.

Yves Congar has been a pioneer—often *the* pioneer—in many of the fields of greatest concern in Catholic theology of the present day. His unrivalled knowledge of the Fathers and the medieval theologians is clear throughout, and he draws on it skilfully to demonstrate the wide range, the full catholicity, and the contemporary relevance of their writing. The individual articles offer some idea of his major contributions in the fields of ecumenism, ecclesiology, hermeneutics, and the theology of the laity.

MARTIN REDFERN

1. Holy Spirit and Spirit of Freedom

"Only in freedom can man direct himself towards goodness. Our contemporaries make much of this freedom and pursue it eagerly; and they are right to do so. Often, however, they foster it perversely as a licence for doing anything they please, even if it is evil. . . . Man's dignity demands that he act according to a knowing and free choice. He achieves that dignity when, emancipating himself from all captivity to passion, he pursues his goal in a spontaneous choice of what is good."—*Pastoral Constitution on the Church in the Modern World*, I, 1, 17.

I want to set before you what the fact of Pentecost means in relation to the theme of Spirit and Freedom. I want to do this in as practical and concrete a fashion as possible; and therefore in a way that touches human life as it is lived. For you are men. What sort of men? Christians, of course, and as such you are citizens of the City that is above, fellow citizens with the blessed in Heaven. But you are also men engaged in the life of this world; and accordingly you seek to live your Easter and your Pentecost, on your own behalf and on behalf of your fellows, in the world of men, on this human earth, here and now. Therefore it is not enough for me to talk about what the Holy Spirit brings to Christian life *in the Church*; I must also show what that Spirit means to Christian life *in the world* as it actually is. And I will begin with that: man, as a child of Easter and Pentecost, in the world of the twentieth century. Afterwards I will speak of man, as a child of Easter and Pentecost, in the Church of the twentieth century—which, of course, is also the Church of all time.

Theologians Today: Yves M. J. Congar

I. IN THE WORLD

Threats to personal freedom

In the first place I must briefly examine man's situation in the world of today from the point of view of our being called to be men of spirit and to be free, and in as much as Christianity concerns this vocation.

There are two outstanding characteristics of the world in which we live that go in opposite directions, and at the same time offset one another: one is the importance given to the individual person and his freedom; the other is the quest for power through organization, with its huge undertakings and a gradual socialization of life.

There is a tendency in modern society to attach an over-riding value to individual freedom. In France especially, freedom is thought of as a right of complete self-government for the individual, the possibility for each person to do what he likes, a freedom limited only by the equal similar freedom of others and by the general will. But, on the other hand, contemporary individuals are at the mercy of two gigantic powers, the nation-state and big industrial enterprise. Material well-being, a good standard of living, has become dependent on large-scale industry, which is more and more based on the use of machinery. Inevitably, this has produced four results that condition our lives; they are these:

    a. Cut-throat competition, which makes life a nerve-racking business at every level. People

today are far too keyed up: they are for ever
trying to go quicker, to overtake a rival, to
pass an exam or get a job that will make them
better off—"better" meaning "ahead of others".

b. The pouring out of an endless stream of propaganda and aggressive publicity that aims at
winning over a huge public, whether in favour
of some manufactured product or a set of ideas
or a political programme. I need not say more
about this; everybody knows it, and it has
often been analysed and denounced: the devices
and resources of propaganda are used to force
human judgment, till eventually people are
unable to think and decide for themselves.

c. Educational institutions with powerful resources, large factories, industrial cities and other
agglomerations: such concentrations of people
of their nature encourage a mass psychology.

d. And then the intervention of public authority,
"the state", responsible for the common good
of its people. This intervention takes the form
of "planning"; it seeks to harmonize the powerful forces on which human well-being depends
in a rational, scientific way. Forecasting of
future conditions and control of factors in them
are based on statistics. And so life becomes
increasingly socialized.,

It is obvious that a common tendency of these four
factors is towards reducing human beings to the state
of a mere mass of creatures. This has been written

about a good deal, particularly by the historian of civilization J. Huizinga. It is his opinion that this "collectivization" of life takes away from man decisions that he ought to make for himself; it dehumanizes him and leaves him a prey to mob characteristics, to cruelty, intolerance, sentimentality, formlessness: in short, to the opposite of what should characterize a human person and a truly humanistic spirit.

It is true that the individual person has reacted against all this, and that the reaction is strong and widespread: but what form does it take, in what direction is it going? Man is in danger of being as it were torn in two, so that the life-blood would be drained away from his inner self and spiritual freedom. There is the risk of letting his life be split into separate compartments: one is his working life, the hard struggle for material existence, planning, all the socialized activities which reduce him to being an item in the general mass; the other is his lesiure time, a counterbalance which he uses to try and tone up his nerves. As soon as he can, he gets away from towns and factories and offices, away to hills and fields and beaches, by car, by bicycle, on foot. Once there, he flings away all the constraint he can (symbolized by the throwing off of clothing). He stops thinking about anything. He has escaped.

But has he not also escaped from himself? What good is it doing him as a man? Freedom for the body, yes; but what about the deeper freedom of the soul, the freedom of a being who is responsible for himself? The danger in this flight from work by wandering, in swapping blouses for bikinis, is that it leaves no room for the human person itself; it is forgotten that there are other needs to be satisfied, such as the things of the mind, spritual freedom, development of one's own character. Is the *whole* man being taken seriously when attention is given only to his job and to keeping up with the Joneses, and to making up for the resulting weariness of spirit by simple diversions and "getting away from it all"?

Some compensations

It must not be forgotten, however, that contemporary life itself includes certain not inconsiderable humanizing resources. In spite of everything, in spite of "statism" and planning and bureaucracy, natural communities have not entirely disappeared: first and foremost there is the family, that great well-spring and sheltering ark of human healthfulness. In those communities man learns his need to protect himself and to associate with others in a more humane way than is provided by benefit-societies or associations arising out of his work. And modern techniques, so far from destroying the worth of certain recreations, spread them abroad and increase their possibilities. I am struck, for instance, by the renewed and big part taken in people's leisure by books, drama, music and singing—these have poetical values, and so spiritual ones. Or again, hiking and camping can contribute to a quest for things of the spirit. And, furthermore, the techniques of the machine, by multiplying ways and means, not only offer new and considerable possibilities of personal culture but strongly encourage their use.

The first stage of the industrial revolution has lasted two hundred years and has now, I hope, touched rock-bottom. It brought into existence a new world of slaves serving machines, and that has resulted in the emergence of a huge body of "hand-to-mouth" wage-earners", a proletariat, a mass of depersonalized individuals without any cultural background. When we find that in some countries nowadays, notably France, the better educated classes have more religious faith and practise it better than the workers as a whole, we are looking at something besides the reflection of economic conditions. Educated people have a personal culture which enables them to attain faith more easily, because they are already acquainted with things of the spirit. This is still the state of affairs for a minority of privileged persons; but it is permissible to think that it will extend to very many more people in the years that lie immediately ahead.

Statistics suggest that this is not a sheer flight of imagination. If the machine sets men free from the necessity of certain toil, automation will do this still more. But there is still the question an Indian is said to have put to an American who boasted of a new machine that would save ten minutes: "And what will you do with the ten minutes?" The existence of this sort of fallacy does not alter the fact that technology by itself is powerful to civilize and humanize. What

Ruskin said is still true, that everything can be made in factories, except men. Nevertheless technology does open a way to an increase of culture. But it is not simply that it reduces human toil: for its own extension and perfecting it requires more better-educated men. In the world today it is *a fact* that, when men leave the natural conditions of primary activities (e.g., agriculture, fishing, forestry), they go less into the secondary activities of industry or building and construction than into the tertiary activities of office work, study, services, school-mastering, the learned and commercial professions. What is happening is what is bound to happen—an ever-increasing extension of what is, on the whole, that middle-class life which is the ambition of every-body everywhere.

So I do not want to ignore the opportunities for "humanization" to be found in our technological world as I have briefly analysed it. But these possibilities are obviously far from denoting a direct and effective increase of the life of the spirit. And indeed the object of this paper is to point out what Easter and Pentecost can do for contemporary man, not only as a remedy for his ills but as a positive principle of life and health.

Man's great need

There are more difficulties in the way of the life of the spirit for man today than for his predecessor in medieval Christendom; and yet he has more need of it. I can hear somebody say: "What? You want to talk about life of the spirit to people harassed like us, who are embroiled in the competition and demands of the world we live in?" And I reply, "Yes. And to them more than any, because they have a very urgent need of it." It is a case where the useless is the most useful, the irrelevant supremely relevant.

A man must have a point deep down in himself in which he can be himself, where he finds and lives his own life. He must as it were inhabit himself. And it is at this inner point that he must find freedom, shaking off and rising above the shackles that constrict his life, including the tyranny of his pleasures (for they can enslave him); but at the same time he keeps his contact with the world of men, for the condition of human life consists, as Maurice Merleau-Ponty has put it, in "being unto the world through a body."

No doubt it could be *proved* by a process of reasoning that only the divine communication which we call the Spirit of God is able to bring this about. But I prefer simply to *assert* that it is so: not on my own "say so", but *as a fact* that is attested by the clearest and most unexceptionable testimony that you can ask for, that of the men and women we call saints. Granted that it is only saints who experience this in the highest degree; but every Christian, every person who is indwelt by God's Spirit, has, or can have, this experience in a lesser way. What this experience is I would express in two sentences reminiscent of, but more philosophical than, Luther's *The Liberty of a Christian Man:* Through the Holy Spirit, the man of Easter and Pentecost is himself, but he is not isolated

18

in himself; he can free himself from the compulsions of his world, while remaining committed to his engagement in its affairs.

The theme of Spirit and Freedom is concerned with man's return to himself, with a refusal of that alienation that would reduce him to being an element in history or in industrial production, free only to compensate for this by "escapes" that reinvigorate the human animal without giving new life to the human person. The man who prays, who knows that God calls him, who is conscious of the divine presence and those divine "touches" that are always accompanied by some demand on us, that man has a personal existence. "The man who prays is never a nobody," said Ernest Hello. Romano Guardini has properly emphasized what may be called the anthropological value, the value for man simply as a man, of recollectedness and—what is obvious enough—of adoring worship.

The same is true of Sunday, in addition to its absolute value as the Lord's Day. It is the day, on which a man or woman stands upright. All the week he or she has, so to speak, been stooping over the ground, at his lathe or his engine or his desk, at her cooking-stove and the children's mending, doing the work of the world. But on this day a man or woman is reminded that he is called to be a citizen of the City that is above; he remembers that he has a soul, and that this makes him a king, above all those things at which he toils like a slave. It has been well said that "The purpose of the Sabbath is to make a breach between man and his functions, to prevent the identification of man with his functions" (Tresmontant), and *in this connection* the same can be said of the Christian Sunday. On this day the Church says to us, completing its message of Ash Wednesday: "Remember, man, that you are spirit and that you will return to the Spirit."

On the one hand, man is subjected to the grinding tyrannies of mass-production and to the indignities of rabbit-warren housing, public transport at the rush-hours, and the rest of it. On the other, he seeks a purely external freedom in inadequate recreations and physical "escapes." But if he has an inner life, if he is an "inward" man, he finds a real self beyond these warring elements. Faced with enslavement to propaganda and advertising, he makes within himself a corner of resistance to the wolves of conformity and mob enthusiasm. The vast increase through technology of means which may be used for the oppression of man by man, for the destruction of man (yes, this includes nuclear weapons) call imperatively for conscientious protests on the same scale. It is absolutely necessary that men should find, in an inner life and the deepest convictions of conscience, means to save their own manhood and that of others.

Faith always makes persons. A religious faith prevents, for example, a worker from being wholly and only a paid "hand", dedicated solely to his work and to the proletarian cause; but this is not so much because such a faith may lead to "bourgeois" or conventional ideas with regard to established authority. Christianity does not prevent him from being a worker or from being active on behalf of workers' interests. But it does make *impossible* that process of reduction, which Marxism exacts and brings about, from man to worker or a means to production, and from worker to proletarian, fully mobilized for service in its class war. Accordingly, though they are not on the same level with it, faith and a religious life are opposed to Marxism: not only doctrinally, in their positive teaching, but in their attitude towards man and what sort of a creature he is. In the same way, though it is not *of* this world, the Christian religion is a power *in* the world. There is an outstanding opportunity for Christians in this age, one of whose greater problems, greater every day, is to harmonize planning with the individual's nature and rights, the social organization of life with the building up and development of persons. But to cope with that, Christians have to to go back to their first principles.

We have got to be very careful, too, that in acquiring depth and an inner self through religion and spiritual life, we do not cut ourselves off from the world. It cannot be denied that there are dangers here: it is a common reproach to us Christians that we selfishly withdraw into a cosy shelter provided by "spiritual" absorption in the needs of our dear little souls. However liberated we may be from the restrictions imposed by a mechanized world, we are still "in the world", with a part to play in its life and history. As Christians, what we need is not *less* spirituality, but more and more of it, and above all a biblical, that is a genuinely Christian, spirituality.

Theories of freedom: the Christian answer

It seems to me that the principal theories of freedom that influence people today can be reduced to three: the idea of it that derives from Rousseau and the Jacobins (particularly influential in France), the Marxist idea, and the Stoic idea.

The first of these looks on freedom as an absolute good, and one to which each individual is entitled: it is only a matter of bringing about the external conditions which encourage its development, and—since it is an absolute good—its greatest possible development. For Marxists, the notion of freedom is simply formal, and ineffectual enough. For them, true freedom is a state that has to be attained through liberation from the "alienations" and hindrances that afflict mankind. It arises from a social situation in which man has been emancipated from oppressive conditions, is conscious that a social plan has been realized in fact, and sees himself as collectively making his own history; he understands everything now and so will never again be put upon by anything or anybody, for his life will be made up only of things that he will do, and will be conscious that he does, collectively.

So, for democracies of the Western type, freedom is something individually owned, and the individual must simply be allowed to use it. For the People's

Republics, it is hoped for as a benefit that is collective as much as personal: the consequence of man's full control of his destiny and of a perfect harmony between man and his labours.

With all their differences, the Rousseauist and Marxist ideas have this in common, that they see freedom as a state of emancipation from constraints that are *outside man himself* and his mind. Making the classical distinction between "freedom *from*" and "freedom *to*", we should say that in this conception of it freedom is essentially a freedom *from*, a right rather than a duty, a liberation from something external to man. Here freedom is not looked on as an inward and positive quality of existence, which is what it is for Christianity. In a way it was for Stoicism too, for Stoicism promoted the notion of freedom as inner independence of whatever can make a man morally a slave. It had its eye particularly on the emotions and disturbances that are provoked in the mind by outside events and nature's contrary ways. The remedy offered was to seek this inner freedom— a personal perfection—through ridding our will of its passions and bringing it into line with the cosmic order of the world, the kind of "general will" diffused in nature. It was a high ideal; and Christianity had sometimes been represented as resembling Stoicism, but in fact it is profoundly different.

Like Stoicism, but to a far greater degree, Christianity refuses to reduce freedom to a matter of free will, the ability to do this or that, the freedom of unconcernedness, or to a liberation from external

23

constraint. Rather is it a spiritual quality of human existence, a perfection or characteristic of man in himself; and, as it actually exists in this or that person, there can be different degrees of it. St Augustine and St Bernard speak of a "freedom from coercion and restraint", freedom to be oneself, to live one's own life; but beyond that of a "freedom from wretchedness", that is, from evil, error and sin, which are more inside ourselves than outside us.

Freedom, then, is not simply freedom from whatever prevents me from ploughing my own furrow in my own way without interference: it is, positively, a matter of our ability to share in goodness and truth. It is, indeed, always a question of man's return to himself, but here man has a pattern that is both above and within himself: to return to self is to return to the image of God. To be rid of some external compulsion is only one degree of freedom, and not the highest. The truth is that man could never be more free than were he by some blessed impossibility, to reach the state of being unable to sin—like God and, in the created order, Christ. (We are a long way from Gide, at the opposite pole in fact.)

The highest degree of freedom is not to govern oneself, but to be wholly governed by God: not forgetting that, while God is outside and above us, he also dwells within us. Because he is God, he is in some sense within us physically; spiritually and morally he is within us through the free gift of his Holy Spirit "in our hearts" (Gal. 4:6). Thus it is *from within*, gently, that he moves us towards what is good, to the true good. The pressure or attraction under whose influence we act is the Holy Spirit himself. Here the whole subject of Christian freedom is involved; and that would entail discussion of the whole "programme" of Christian life and the Christian ethic as a *paschal*, an Easter programme, concerned with the achievement of spiritual freedom. "A price was paid to redeem you; do not enslave yourselves!" (1 Cor. 7:23; cf. 6:20; 7:22; Gal. 5:1).

The essential and distinguishing thing in the Christian teaching about freedom, differentiating it from Soicism, is that it takes account, not of two factors, but of three. Not simply man and those circumstances external to man that eventually enslave and tyrannize over him; but man, external circumstances, God. And it is God that makes all the difference. Stoicism tried to find freedom through ridding our will of its passions (*apatheia*) and bringing it into line with the general will of nature, the world's cosmic order. The Christian's cosmos is quite different: it is not a world of cosmic nature, but a world of God's designing, of the free saving design that the living God follows therein.

Accordingly, Christian freedom consists in the perfect agreement, not of an "apathetic" will with nature, but of a love-intoxicated will with the saving will of God as it is shown forth in Jesus Christ. "Philip, whoever has seen me, has seen the Father. ... I am the way" (Jn. 14:9, 6).

Theologians Today: Yves M. J. Congar

True religion is not isolating

Now this will of God, in action, as we see it in Jesus our way, is love and service, the humble service of love; it is love coming into this world to take its evil on itself and to overcome it in the manner of the Suffering Servant (cf. Isaiah 52:13–53:12 etc.) it is what St Paul calls "the wisdom of the Cross".

In those meaningful symbolic images that the thirteenth century was so fond of, Free Will was sometimes represented climbing a ladder, and the ladder was Christ's cross. Adam thought, Sartre thinks, we all think in our unregenerate moods, that the way of freedom is the way of self-will. It is not. It is the way of dependence, of lowliness, of giving oneself to others. Freedom is made real only in love: not in being "for myself", wrapped up in self, but in being "for others" and "going out" to them. . . . If it be taken in its properly Christian meaning, surely it is right to say that the life of the spirit, so far from isolating us, ensures that we live "in the world"— and that we do so freely.

But who dare believe so firmly in that as to act accordingly? Who dare stake his all, his whole life, on the Gospel's "He that shall lose his life for me shall find it"? Who dare lose himself in Jesus Christ, believing that so he will find himself again? Who dare give himself in the certainty that thus he will possess himself, and rise above himself for love's sake with the assurance that thus will he be free?

2. IN THE CHURCH

The Holy Spirit and the Church

The Spirit of Pentecost created the Church, or rather, gave life and impetus to it; he launched it into the world as something in the world but not of it, having a mission to the world, with an existence and a life of its own, given from on high: made up of men, and yet a divine institution.

It is a little like the work of natural creation as it is presented in the book of Genesis: God first makes a being of a certain kind, and then gives it life; or like Ezekhiel's vision of the valley of dry bones: God brings together the scattered bones to make skeletons, he clothes them with sinews and flesh, and then he breathes life into them. So it was with the Church. First it was given form. That was the work of Jesus Christ during his public ministry: he chose and sent out the twelve apostles, he revealed the Father and announced the good news of the Kingdom, he instituted the sacraments thanks to which we were to share in his mystery through the contacts of our senses. So the essential lines of the Church were laid, the building was in place, the body ready. There only remained to give it breath and life: that was the work of the Holy Spirit.

So we see that the making of the Church involved two "moments" or stages. This is a fundamental point for our subject, and it is important to get a proper grasp of it. I will first explain it from the standpoint of principles, showing the Holy Spirit's relation to Christ; and then from the standpoint of activity, what that Spirit does in the Church.

Christ is one divine person, the Holy Spirit is another, a person in himself (cf. Jn 14:16f.); but he is the Spirit *of Christ*, the Spirit *of the Son* (Spirit of Christ: Rom 8:9; 1 Pet 1:11. Spirit of the Lord: Acts 5:9; 8:39; 2 Cor 3:17–18. Spirit of Jesus: Acts 16:7; Rom 8:9–11; Phil 1:19. Spirit of the Son: Gal 4:6.) Thus the Holy Spirit has a "mission", a "coming", of his own: just as the Father sent the Son into this world and the Son came in Jesus Christ, so the Father sends the Holy Spirit to dwell in those who follow Christ. But the work of the Holy Spirit's mission is not *his* work, something independent and self-contained: it is the work *of Christ*, who has already done the Father's work, given the Father's message. . . . The Spirit consecrates and sanctifies *Christ's* apostles; he gives them understanding of what *Christ* taught them ("The truth-giving Spirit . . . will not utter a message of his own. . . . He will recall to your minds everything I have said to you": Jn 16:13; 14:26); he makes men holy through *Christ's* sacraments.

If we look at the Holy Spirit's work and activities we notice two points that take us to the heart of this second part of our subject. The first point is that: *The Holy Spirit is sent into men's hearts; he makes Christianity intimate and personal.*

With the help of the Bible we can (as the early Fathers did) apportion the various parts of God's work among the divine persons of the Blessed Trinity; and we then see what can be called, in human terms, an ever-deepening and closer concern of God with his creatures.

There is first of all the Creation, the making of the world and of all things, visible and invisible: this we can attribute to the Father, who overrules all. "I believe in one God, the almighty Father, maker of heaven and earth", says the *Credo*, which is built up on the threefold pattern of the Trinity. Then there is the Redemption, the work of the Son. This too, is in a way, an external work. The Son is sent *into the world*, and he there establishes a means of salvation as an objective fountain of grace. At the prayer and in the name of the Son, the Father sends the Holy Spirit in order that this life may be made ours.

We are told that the Son was sent into the world, but that the Holy Spirit is sent "into our hearts". (Gal 4:4–6.) His particular part is to bring to the heart of each one of us the work that Christ did objectively for all. The Holy Spirit, the third and last of the divine persons of the Trinity, is the bond, in God, of that inter-flow of life that constitutes the fellowship of the Three in oneness; and it is for him to apply Christ's work to each of us, to bring personally to the heart of each and every Christian Christ's grace, Christ's love, Christ's mind, Christ's power.

The second point is that: *The Holy Spirit is given to the Church; we receive him only in the fellowship of the whole.*

29

While the Holy Spirit makes Christianity inward and personal, he is given to the whole Church, as Church, to be its unifying principle. He is in each member, intimately with each, but he is one and the same in all. J. A. Möhler pointed out that the Spirit was given to the disciples just when they were all together and of one mind in prayer and love. Jesus had already said that "Where two or three are gathered together in my name, I am there in the midst of them" (Mt 18:20).

The Spirit then is given to each, but in company with the rest. He is the principle of unity, as the soul is for the different parts of the human organism. He dwells within each person, in his heart or spirit, as the inner law of fellowship and unity. My soul is not given to my hand apart from my head or my heart. If my members are separated one from another, they cease to live. Just so he who is the principle of personal faith and individual Christian life is given us within a unified organism and for a unifying purpose. The office of the Holy Spirit is precisely to bring together in unity the gifts that he implants in individual persons.

After all, we already know that, from the Christian point of view, a person fulfils himself and attains freedom by "going out" and giving himself to others, in a spirit of humble ministering love. Every time St Paul speaks of the charisms, the spiritual gifts, with which the inner life of Christians is so richly endowed, he emphasizes their variousness, but shows that they are given through the members of the Body for the use and benefit of all (1 Cor 12; Rom 12; Eph 4). The Spirit is indeed the living principle of personal religion; but he is given to each man or woman as a member of an organic whole and according to the part each has to take or the contribution that he or she has to make to the unique life of that Body. In this way Christianity brings together two things that are often in opposition to one another: "inwardness" or personal life, and the communal principle or unity.

Suppose it is a question of the public and institutional aspect of the Church. Then, if you are one of the lay faithful, you have been given the Spirit that you may believe; if you are a bishop, you have been given the Spirit that you may be a shepherd, to care for and direct the flock that the Holy Spirit has entrusted to you (Acts 20:28). Or is it a question of the hidden life of the soul? One person has the grace of prayer, and uses it for the good of others; a second person has the grace of strength or of giving testimony or of comforting: hiddenly, through the working of the Holy Spirit, these are all brought together to do Christ's work in that communion of saints in which we declare our belief in the *Credo*.

I have already quoted Merleau-Ponty to the effect that man has to "be unto the world through a body". Could not the situation of the Christian be characterized as "belonging to God through, by means of, and in the organic unity of a Church"?—the Church that is People of God and Body of Christ. . . .

We can now understand why, where Christian life is concerned, the man of Easter and Pentecost is

31

faced both by an unquestionable duality and by the necessity of unity.

We cannot deny a certain duality or push it out of sight; we often meet it, expressed in different words and from different points of view: communalism and mysticism, static and dynamic, closed and open, letter and spirit, institution and event, legality and spiritual gifts, official and personal, priestly and prophetical, and who knows what else. There is a duality because there are two missions, that of Christ and that of the Holy Sprit; but we know these two missions are for one and the same work. To deny one or other of the two terms is not the answer; the answer is to hold fast to both in their unity and to make their harmony with one another real to ourselves, for that is the nature of God's work.

The religion of Pentecost is *at the same time* the religion of inward Spirit and of Church, of direct "contact" and of mediation. Not to recognize that, to see only a purely inward, personal and direct relationship of religious people with God, is to fail to recognize the true religious relation as God has revealed it and shown it forth in and through Jesus Christ. And, on the other hand, to pass over the element of personal inwardness, and stress and pay attention to the institutional side alone, is to ignore an authentic aspect of God's work and of the Christian reality.

What this means for the laity

There is no doubt whatever—and it has been remarked on more than once lately—that not enough has been heard about this personal aspect of religion; or at any rate that it has been too much confined to the personal life of prayer and union with God. Too little is said about its various significances in the Church's life: Christian freedom, its part in the maintaining and development of doctrine, initiative in the Church, the whole business of the laity's "coming of age." Like all omissions of the kind, the frequent ignoring of such matters sometimes provokes people to seek compensation in irresponsible fault-finding, a sort of flirtation with freedom, which is rather unhealthy. Are we going to leave the privilege of meeting these aspirations to Christian bodies that are not Catholic, and so cause much harm to the truth of an authentic religious relationship?

The important truth that emerges from what has been said above, and which must guide us in what remains to be said, is this: Lay people are not only *objects* in the Church, objects though they are of her goodness and care; they are also religious *subjects*, and therefore active persons. They are not only *made by* the Church, in as much as the Church is a hierarchical institution; they *make* the Church, in as much as it is *congregatio fidelium*, the society of the faithful, as the Church was defined in the middle ages. That the laity are personal subordinate subjects is true; it is also true that they must conform themselves to the Church's unity, a unity that has its own structure, rules and requirements. But this unity is not that of a merely external association (such as a club): it is the unity of a body living in all its parts, of a fellowship, a communion of persons.

In short, a Christian is not simply a bit of the material on which the Church works, any more than a man is simply a bit of the material of history or of industrial production or of governmental power. Every person exists in himself, he has a destiny of his own, that he cannot relinquish to anybody else. But it must be observed, in passing, that this does not work out in exactly the same way in civil society and in the Church. The proper and specific object of the Church is the *supernatural* destiny of persons; but this is not the case with civil society.

Lay people, then, are persons in the Church. With truly Roman precision and conciseness, canon law declares: "By baptism a man becomes a person in Christ's Church, with every Christian right and duty" (Canon 87). Being a juridical document it understands "person" in a juridical sense, as the subject of rights and duties; and that is useful for our purpose. The Church says that the Christian has the rights and duties of a person: among them, the rights and duties of freedom are certainly not the least. These are our concern; so let us look at them from two points of view, that of inner freedom, a deep personal quality, and that of external freedom.

For lay people the essential point is the duty, and the corresponding right, to become *adult Christians, free men.* These two terms are practically equivalent. A free man is one who governs his own actions, who does not submit to other pressure than that of his own choice. *"Liber est causa sui"*, says St Thomas Aquinas, following Aristotle: the free man is the self-determined man. But the adult—I am of course referring to moral and spiritual adulthood, a state to which the grown-up in years does not always attain—the adult is a man who no longer has to be warned, encouraged, supervised in order that he may act. When we were children we went to Mass because we were told to. Plenty of grown men and women go simply because they fear "what the neighbours might say" or because of the reproofs that will fall on them if they do not. The spiritual adult goes because he knows what he is about and has personal spiritual convictions within himself that move him to go. And so he goes freely.

To be a Christian with an adult faith is a very big commitment. On the negative side, for example, it involves putting away attitudes and behaviour that are childish, mechanical, legalistic, governed more or less by *taboos* and apprehensions that are more reminiscent of the religions of heathernism than of faith in the living God, the God, "who is, and ever was, and is still to come" (Rev 1:4; Exod 3:14). And here I believe is the crux of the whole matter—faith in the living God. This is not the place to set out the reasons; but I am convinced, after much thought about it, that the real key to an adult Christianity is to be found in living faith—not some "religious attitude" or other—and in faith in the living God—not in some celestial Leader, Eternal Axiom, Great Architect or Supreme Being.

35

The need for adult Christians

I have two more deep-seated convictions in this
matter. One is that the age we are living in has a
special need for such Christians. Fr. E. Mersch has
written nicely that "some animals need a shell
because they have not got a skeleton". If this be
true, we may well think that Catholics need to be
given a strong spiritual skeleton, when we look
around and see on all hands that the old sociological
frameworks of Catholicism are being called in question, shaken loose and damaged by modern conditions
and events.

A Christendom that is going to renew itself and
live in the present cannot, apart from rare survivals,
start from a basis of regulations, social set-ups, the
favour of public authority, social pressure, as was
the case in the past. It has to start from personal
conviction, from the witness and glowing influence of Christians who are such from their very
depths. The time has gone by nearly everywhere
when civil powers would pay attention to priestly
authority expressed in terms of that authority. But
Christian witness, arising from the convictions of a
conscience dedicated to the living God, is as strong
as ever: yes, even against the powers of the world,
as we saw, for instance, in Germany when the
Protestants of the "Confessing Church" stood out
against Hitler in the name of their faith in Christ,
who alone is Lord. For that we need really adult
Christians, free men who have been set free by
Truth (Jn 8:32).

But I am also convinced that this to a great extent depends on the clergy. Only an adult priesthood can increase the number of adult lay people. There can be no witness from the laity unless the priesthood comes up to the ideal (to the best of its ability—the finest of us are but poor creatures!) expressed by the rector of a seminary: "I do not want to turn my students into clerics who have the spirit of Levites, but into priests who have the spirit of prophets."

As things are, do not ecclesiastics often seem more ready to give orders than to educate, to insist than to uplift? In my *Lay People in the Church* I have quoted several statements from Catholics on this score; here I want to quote a critic from outside, whose words are nevertheless worth pondering. This is what Amiel wrote in his *Journal:*

> Catholic thought cannot conceive personality as conscious and master of itself. Its daring and its weakness come from the same cause: lack of responsibility, subjection of conscience, which knows only slavery or an anarchy that proclaims the law but does not obey it because it is outside itself. . . . "Right-wing" Catholicism never gives its followers freedom: they have to accept, believe and obey, because they never grow up.

There is more than one ambiguity in that passage; it is a caricature, and false accordingly: but it is worth thinking about for all that.

It can hardly be denied that, in taking a side or expressing an opinion, Catholics often try to shelter behind some authority, some law or decision or extract from an encyclical letter or papal address: in other words, they try to find a shell. Is it because they have no skeleton, no backbone, no nerves, no muscles? When I saw a fine film about Maxim Gorky's younger days I was struck by a sentence that occurred in it twice. "Be careful never to shelter your conscience behind somebody else's conscience." If you want to hear the verdict of an orthodox Catholic, and a cardinal at that, read Newman's answer to Gladstone about papal infallibility; he explains how the pope's authority, so far from annulling the individual conscience, presupposes the strength and faithfulness of that conscience, and he ends humorously:

> Certainly, if I am obliged to bring religion into after-dinner toasts (which indeed does not seem quite the thing), I shall drink—to the Pope, if you please—still to Conscience first and to the Pope afterwards.

That is to say, it is the honouring of the first toast that would give meaning and value to the second.

Among the Church tasks and pastoral undertakings I would give the formation of Christian *men* precedence over organizations and systematic groupings. To be sure, such things are wanted; but we ought never to forget what our Lord told the Pharisees, that "The sabbath was made for man, not man for the sabbath": we have to appreciate the significance of those words for Church matters, as well as their

38

moral truth. In the middle ages they were fond of expressing the same idea in the words "The Church is not the walls but the faithful"; and I would like here to recall a remark of Bernanos: "It is a fine thing to put social programmes on paper. But it is important to know what sort of people you have to carry them out." For the Church, indeed, that is the main question. Pope Pius XII declared that the Church's influence differs from that of political societies through the fact that "it acts on man in his personal dignity as a free being at his very heart; it strives to form men . . ., and it does its work in the depths of each one".

Everybody knows that it is difficult to make men free. Often they are the first not to want to be free; having to make their own decisions is a heavy burden, and they like other people to do it for them, as Dostoyevsky set out so forcefully in "The Legend of the Grand Inquisitor" in *The Brothers Karamazov.* Yes, it is difficult to make men free—and it is risky, too. Many do not know how to use their freedom, and some know too well how to abuse it. But there are risks naturally attaching to the use of freedom even short of real misuse. Freedom calls for open discussion and frank give-and-take: it is therefore a threat to dogmatism (I do not say "to dogma"!). Freedom involves the acceptance sometimes of un-certainties and hazards; these are things that alarm a short-sighted authority, or one that is too self-conscious, an authority that is inclined to "patern-alism". And, even when it works within the limits

39

that it must not over-step, the spirit of freedom cannot fail to express itself outwardly in certain dissentient attitudes that insist on asking questions.

Freedom in the Church

I have just said "within the limits that it must not over-step". The faithful Christian has to be free *in* the Church, but not *with regard to* the Church, that is to say, not with regard to the essential things of that institution which Jesus Christ founded for our salvation: dogma, sacraments, apostolic authority, unity in the faith. We are free in the truth; it is, indeed, the truth that makes us free (Jn 8:32); but we are not free with regard to the truth. Please keep this well in mind: it is fundamental to what I am now going to say, which is concerned chiefly with the Christian's external freedom in the Church.

First I want to call your attention to that great field in the Church today, as at every other time, wherein Catholics enjoy extremely wide spiritual freedom. It is something very real and positive; and if some people are hardly conscious of it, it is perhaps because they are not much concerned about the life of the spirit and of charity. Please just think what scope there is for *religious initiative* in the Church. Within the sacred limits of unity in the faith and communion with the successors of the apostles, you are free, not only to pray how you like, to sing your spiritual song to your own tune, but also to undertake some apostolic work or other: if you want to, you can found a new religious congregation, and give it a striking habit or the quaintest of head-dresses. I am not joking! There is no end to the originality of the saints, whom the Church celebrates individually, each under his or her own name.

Recognition has always been given in the Church to what would be called in English the law of conscience: its traditional name is *lex privata Spiritus Sancti*, the individual or "private" law of the Holy Spirit, as distinguished from *lex canonum*, the eternal law that applies to everybody. It was recognized that the relations of a man's conscience with God go beyond the bounds of his relationship with the Church's canonical organs. A person has spiritual aspects which are not reducible to terms of ecclesiastical common form.

At the same time there was and is always in the Church the fundamental principle that I have set before you: the Holy Spirit is the Spirit *of Christ*. He does not come to do some new and different work, but to do that work whose essential elements have been fixed by the Word made flesh. There is now law of the Spirit which can go against these essential things, no "inner voice" that can truthfully gainsay Christ's own work: "No one can be speaking through God's Spirit if he calls Jesus accursed" (1 Cor 12:3).

Let us glance at the question of freedom of speech and public opinion in the Church. Here the documentation is again very extensive and includes, as well as private writers, the utterance of weighty official authorities. So, in contradiction of what I

41

have just said, I can shelter my conscience behind other people's! But I am sure you will appreciate that the subject is one of special importance and delicacy.

I quote, therefore, the synodal statutes of the Archdiocese of Cologne of 1954:

> Lay persons are not fobidden to protest against the shortcomings of members of the clergy, by a brotherly remonstrance and with a due sense of their own deficiences.

Then I appeal not to Caesar, but to a pope. In 1950 Pius XII declared that public opinion is an attribute of every normal society made up of people who are conscious of their responsibilities, and that the absence of a free public opinion would be a disease in social life. He went on briefly to apply these truths to the Church, "for she is a living body," he said, "and something would be lacking to her life were there no public opinion in it, a want for which the blame would rest on pastors and faithful". Finally, I invoke the Vatican II *Constitution on the Church* (IV, 37):

> An individual layman, by reason of the knowledge, competence, or outstanding ability which he may enjoy, is permitted and sometimes even obliged to express his opinion on things which concern the good of the Church.

Freedom of speech in the Church is, of course, only one chapter in the whole business of making religion personal. In a short space I can only pick and choose my topics; and it is with full consciousness of being deplorably "bitty" that I select, to end with, one of the chief enemies of this personal undertaking and ideal—juridicism or legalism.

Freedom and legalism

I repeat with emphasis what I have said about the relation of the Spirit to the foundations, faith and sacraments and apostolic institution, that were given by the incarnate Word. And I am not attacking either law of its enactments—I believe it would take a lot of torture to make me utter a single word against canon law itself. It is true that the spiritual man is emancipated from the law as law, that is, from an external coercive obligation, because by love he has made it an inward, personal thing. But in as much as God is not yet "all in all" (to use St Paul's unsearchably deep expression), we stand in need of the discipline of an outward law; with St Thomas Aquinas, we must look on it as a wholesome aid to the spiritual self and our efforts to deepen it. Fron this standpoint, a strictly theological value can be given to Newman's explanation of the considerable increase, in modern times, of doctrinal and disciplinary action by ecclesiastical authority, especially by the central authority. Rationalism, atheism and the anarchy of thought, he said, demanded this strengthening of the Church's teaching and controlling authority; and this power, he added, "viewed in its fullness, is as tremendous as the giant evil which has called for it" (*Apologia pro vita sua*).

The Church's law is holy, its authority is holy; but they exist for the benefit of the spiritual life of the Church's members. Once again, the Church is not walls, or barriers either, but people, the faithful. St Thomas teaches that the Christian law consists principally (and his "principally" has very nearly the meaning of "essentially") in the inward grace of the Holy Spirit; secondarily, and as auxiliary to and in the service of the first, in the external things, dogma, sacraments, authority, rules and the rest (*ST* i–ii, 2. 108, a.1).

Juridicism or legalism results from forgetting, at any rate in practice, this relationship of service and subordination: an absolute value is given to what are means to an end, such importance is attached to them that in practice everything seems to revolve round their observance. It is well known that forms, "correctness", tend to acquire an inflated value and to be mistaken for the whole of religion. The Church's history records one reform movement after another: and these reforms sprang up, precisely, in the name of the *meaning* of things, as against undue concern about rubrics or observances; or in the name of the Gospel, as against the temptation to exclusiveness and pharisaism. In our individual lives, but also in the life of the totality of us gathered in the *Ecclesia*, there is need for a perpetual revision of means, in the light of how those means originated and of the ends to which they are directed. At this very time this is happening in a most striking and effective way in the field of public worship.

We must always beware lest *legal* aspects are allowed to capture and monopolize *spiritual* matters. This can in practice lead to regarding orthodoxy as essentially a defence of the clergy's authority, and to exalting obedience as *the* virtue of the good Catholic. The Church is sometimes looked on too much as an external, juridical society, one in which the characteristic relations are those of authority with its subjects, of subordinates with their rulers. Of course this is one aspect of the Church; but the Church has it *after its own fashion*, and its most characteristic and searching laws are those required by communities of persons, in particular the sort of community that is a *communion* or *fellowship*—a fellowship of life, of salvation, of sanctification and of witness, a fellowship of which the Holy Spirit is the personal indwelling principle.

Such a community of men on this earth needs rules and regulations, an authority, the relations proper to a society. But all that is to minister to and help the spiritual life of persons, and it must not weigh too heavily or be excessive. Laws that are too burdensome are apt to produce rebels or hypocrites or people whose character is infantile. Too many regulations and external obligations, said St Augustine, do not accord with man's condition according to the Gospel, which is that of son, not of slave; St Thomas and the whole of the middle ages echoed Augustine, and the same idea was voiced at the Council of Trent. In all this the Church has constantly to contend against its natural or human element, so that

45

it may be obedient to the Spirit of Christ; that Spirit which, acting in it and in each of its members, bishops, priests and laity, is so profoundly its own.

A problem for everybody

One last remark. What I have been saying might give a superficial hearer or reader the impression that, in the Church, the quest for freedom of spirit is a sort of concealed conflict between those below and the "higher-ups". It is not so. Spiritual freedom is a question of *Christian existence*; the rulers in the Church are in the first place Christians, and they have to face the question as much as do those who are ruled, each at his own level. St Augustine used to say to his flock, using those verbal alliterations of which he was so fond: *Vobis sum episcopus, vobiscum christianus* ("I am bishop over you, but I am Christian with you").

I appeal to you to think about what I have said in the light in which I have said it all through from the beginning: the light, that is, of the Holy Spirit, the gift of Easter and of Pentecost, the soul of the Body of Christ; the Spirit that breathes in each member of that Body according to what he or she is, the faithful as being subordinate "in Christ", the rulers as being our leaders "in the Lord". There is no question of a capricious, irresponsible freedom, an unregenerate freedom; each of us shares in the freedom of Christ's Easter and his Pentecost in proportion to our dedication to him, to the degree that we are bound to him. To be God's servant, that is the only Christian freedom.

2. Scripture, Revelation, Church and Tradition

"Christ the Lord, in whom the full revelation of the supreme God is brought to completion, commissioned the apostles to preach to all men. . . . In order to keep the Gospel for ever whole and alive within the Church, the apostles left bishops as their successors, 'handing over their own teaching role' to them. . . . The words of the holy Fathers witness to the living presence of this tradition, whose wealth is poured into the practice and life of the believing and praying Church."
—*Dogmatic Constitution on Divine Revelation*, II, 7 and 8.

1. *Scripture's sufficiency. We seek, and find, every-thing in it. All theological and pastoral activity flows from it*

St Paul wrote as follows to Timothy:

> From childhood you have been acquainted with the sacred writings which are able to instruct you for salvation through faith in Christ Jesus. All scripture is inspired by God and profitable for teaching, for reproof, for correction, and for training in righteousness, that the man of God may be complete, equipped for every good work. (2 Tim 3:15–17).

St Paul was referring to the prophetic writings in this passage, but if we add to them the writings of the apostolic age, we can say that this has remained the programme for the whole Christian spiritual tradition.

The Fathers did not regard Scripture only as a source of knowledge: for them it is the very principle of salvation and perfection, in short, of Christian living. For them, indeed, there was hardly a meaningful distinction between knowledge and salvation: still less an opposition between the two. The Christ-

ians of the first two centuries had a vivid sense of the
light brought by the scriptural revelation to a dark-
ling world; this is a frequent theme of their thanks-
giving prayers. They appreciated the intellectual side
of this knowledge, but were more conscious of it as
wisdom, wherein *knowledge* and *value* were both
united as instruction and a guide for living. Antiquity
was familiar with the constant search for wisdom;
and the Christians, for their part, acquired, in
Scripture, the sovereign treasure of the true philo-
sophy and a total wisdom, leading to the ultimate
goal of the blessed life. Men had, throughout their
history, made numerous efforts to escape from their
misery; this it was that had spurred on research in
the arts and sciences. They did not succeed; but
God had come to their aid, and had given them his
own Wisdom in Scripture.

Scripture was at once a source of knowledge and a
key to salvation. Thus the Fathers attribute to it
effects in the spiritual life which we should usually
ascribe to grace. Scripture frees from vainglory, says
St John Chrysostom, it cures and consoles. Ignorance
of Scripture is the cause of all evils. We are saved
by it, and should not be saved without it. (*PG* 62,
359–62.) Origen, Jerome, Gregory the Great, express
themselves similarly. They speak of Scripture as if it
achieved the whole reconstitution of man in the
image of God, the whole of the spiritual life from the
initial purifications to the divine union. Modern
authors, too—Closen, Charlier, Stählin, etc.—show
how Scripture contains a principle for our com-

munion with God: it communicates Christ to us, thus taking on a sacramental character.

Thus it is in a very real sense that Scripture contains everything, according to the Fathers and the medieval writers; in it, God has given us everything necessary or useful for the conduct of our lives. It includes in itself the whole of saving truth. Hence, so convinced of this were some writers that they did not hesitate to suppose that what was true in Plato's writings must have been borrowed from the books of Moses. Scripture contains the whole of the mystery of Christ, and thus the whole of "the power of God and the wisdom of God" (1 Cor 1:24). Our analytical approach has lost something of the freshness with which the Fathers were able to see the very presence of Christ assimiliating us to himself: the body of Christ, in fact. It is through Scripture that Christians are what they are.

Scripture is the rule of faith, and of truth, as St Augustine says. This is the reason why patristic theology is purely and simply the study of the sacred writings: the Fathers are essentially *tractatores, expositores sacrae Scripturae.* Throughout the Middle Ages the Bible was the textbook for theological teaching, and its ceasing, eventually, to play this role entailed a subsequent decadence in theological thought.

2. *Scripture is not self-explanatory: heretics have always appealed to it, while differing among themselves*
At an early date the Church encountered heresies

whose authors invariably took their stand on Scripture, often claiming to recognize this as the sole court of appeal; thus the Arians, Pelagians, Monophysites— in fact, all heretics, as Origen had already noted, and after him Sts Hilary and Cyril of Alexandria, then, against Wycliffe, Thomas Netter, and, arguing against Luther, the Catholic controversialists, Thomas More, Driedo, Stapleton, and much later, Möhler, etc.

From the earliest times, the defenders of the Catholic faith accused the heretics of misuse of Scripture. They often reproached them with a material corruption of the scriptural texts. In especial, it was argued that they distorted the Scriptures, perverting their meaning by reading into them their own personal and erroneous ideas. Irenaeus and Tertullian compared the heretics' treatment of Scripture to the making of centos from scraps of Homer. Tertullian not only reproached heretics with misuse of Scripture, but even categorically denied them the right to handle in a way other than the Church's own what is in fact the legitimate property of the Church alone. Origen, like Tertullian, held that heretics steal the divine words from the Church in order to give them an alien meaning: this is, he said, a kind of spiritual adultery. "The devil himself has quoted Scripture texts," says St Jerome; "we could all, while preserving the letter of Scripture, read into it some novel doctrine." (*PL* 23, 182 A.) St Augustine, likewise, argues that heretics are wrong because they misread scriptural texts which are themselves good, and which they are quite right to value highly (*PL* 33, 459.) This is a common patristic theme, found alike in writings on heresy or on Scriptures and it is further to be encountered frequently in the Middle Ages.

It is also emphasized that heretics fail to agree among themselves. Lack of unity in faith is in itself a sign of error: Thomas Netter pointed this out against Wycliffe's disciples, and it was widely used by the Catholic apologists against the Reformers, but St Vincent of Lerins had already drawn the conclusion that it is necessary to adhere to a reading of Scripture which is directed "secundum ecclesiastici et catholici sensus normam". He wrote, in 434:

Here, perhaps, someone may ask: Since the canon of the Scripture is complete and more than sufficient in itself, why is it necessary to add to it the authority of ecclesiastical interpretation? As a matter of fact, [we must answer] Holy Scripture, because of its depth, is not universally accepted in one and the same sense. The same text is interpreted differently by different people, so that one may almost gain the impression that it can yield as many different meanings as there are men. Novatian, for example, expounds a passage in one way; Sabellius, in another; Donatus, in another. Arius, and Eunomius, and Macedonius read it differently; so do Photinus, Apollinaris, and Priscillian; in another way, Jovinian, Pelagius, and Caelestius; finally, in still another way, Nestorius. Thus, because of the great distortions caused by various errors, it is, indeed, necessary that the trend of the interpretation of the prophetic and apostolic writings be directed in accordance with the rule of the ecclesiastical and Catholic meaning. [*PL* 50, 639.]

The argument here is brief and to the point. The fact that all authors of new doctrines appeal to the Bible and yet fail to agree among themselves proves that the preservation of the faith is not governed simply by the individual's reading of Scripture, even presupposing the interior guidance of the Holy Spirit: what is required is Church guidance, the Catholic sense, or the ecclesial understanding of Scripture, which we spoke of earlier. Present-day theology has further developed the notion of the assisted magisterium's regulative role in the Catholic sense and interpretation of Scripture: in short, the Church must itself be counted among the regulating elements of its own belief. We must add here that this holds good not only for Scripture but equally for the witnesses of Tradition: for heretics have also at times appealed to the Fathers or to an early stage in the history of institutions or of doctrine, as can be seen in the case of Berengar of Trous, the Jansenists, and the Old Catholics.

The trouble is that there are two elements in Scripture: the letter and the meaning. The letter poses a problem to begin with, for why do we accept *this* particular piece of writing as normative and not another? We shall return to this later, in

54

speaking of the canon of Scripture. The meaning or sense of Scripture also presents us with a difficulty: it is distinct from the letter, *Scripturae enim non in legendo sunt, sed in intelligendo* ("the Scriptures depend, not on their being read, but on their being understood" [*PL* 10, 570 A]); and it does not follow on as a matter of course as soon as we have determined the letter. Was it not a medieval saying that *auctoritates* have wax noses, which could be bent to right or left as preferred? Duns Scotus, for example, admitted that the letter of the eucharistic texts in the New Testament did not seem to him, of itself, to impose transubstantiation as an explanation: this is rather a clarification due to the *sensus Ecclesiae*, celebrating and living the mystery, and to its assisted magisterium This is the conclusion we must come to once we have seen that Scripture is not sufficient of itself to found belief.

Luther denied this conclusion, though quite well aware that heretics or "enthusiasts" (*Schwärmer*) would also make their appeal to Scripture, just as he had done but—against him. While still a Catholic, Luther stressed the necessity of a living teaching. Without *in fact* abandoning this necessary complement, as an indispensable counter-weight to freakish interpretations, he later insisted upon the self-authenticating character which Scripture possesses in virtue of its essential content, Christ and his saving grace. "Every spirit which does not confess Jesus is not of God" (1 Jn 4:3). Scripture presents itself as speaking of Christ: this is the "analogy of

faith" (Rom 12:6), that is, the pointing of the
relationship, or, the reference on the strength of
which an interpretation proves itself authentic or
otherwise. The interpretation that declares or con-
fesses Christ is authentic, but Christ is confessed in
truth when no human works are placed above or
against his grace, that is to say, when one adopts the
criterion of salvation by faith alone. Luther thus
found *within* Scripture a criterion which would
respect, which would even presuppose and declare
its "sufficiency" and its "transparency".

We are agreed on this idea of the "analogy of
faith", but think it an insufficient criterion: for to
accept it would be to suppose that the problem had
been already solved. It is quite true that Scripture
(or what amounts to the same, revelation, faith)
must refer as a whole to the Christian mystery, or
to the covenant relationship established by God in
Jesus Christ: this will be examined further in the
rest of this chapter. But the key, question is how
exactly we may know whether what the Church says,
for example, about Mary, and the sacraments, etc.,
belongs or does not belong to this covenant relationship as established in Jesus Christ, and inherited in
full by the Church from the apostles. It is the content
itself, which Luther wishes to take as a criterion,
which is in question here: and it is of *this* content
that we speak when we say that it can only be
preserved and known in the Church, by receiving it
from the Church and living it in the Church, and
therefore, by finding it in Scripture. We thus return

to the traditional position of St Vincent of Lerins and (in this matter) of Tertullian who justified on this ground his use of the argument of prescription: "Wherever it is obvious that the truth of Christian doctrine and faith resides, there also will be found true Scripture, true interpretations and all the true Christian traditions." (*Sources Chrétiennes*, 46.)

3. *The meaning of Scripture must be communicated by the Spirit of God in a revelatory action whose fruit in us is Christian knowledge, "gnosis"*

The Fathers and medieval theologians believed that God had placed in Scripture, once and for all, the whole of wisdom. But as God alone is able fully to understand what he has said, he alone can enable us to understand in our turn: Scripture must be read by the light of the same Spirit as has inspired its writing. As long as the human race lasts, there must correspond to that perfect act which God posited once and for all in giving the Scripture to men, an activity on God's part by which he confers upon them a growing understanding of the meaning and content of his Word. Scripture is inspired, it contains the truth, but its content and meaning must be disclosed or revealed to us. In this sense, for the Fathers and medieval writers, the canonical Scriptures are not revelation: revelation (or inspiration) in their vocabulary does not designate a mere objective deposit, but rather an act: the act by which God communicates to us the knowledge of what he thinks or wills. This can be the name of the person to whom God wishes to entrust the priestly or royal ministry; it can be a particular detail in the matter of sacramental rites or in what we call casuistry; it can also be the meaning of sacred Scripture, or many other things besides. Whatever the matter in question, there must be a fully "theonomic" manner of living, under God's guidance, in which we wait until he makes known (*revelare*) his thought or will. We must not await this activity in a purely passive, quietist, manner. God intervenes as he wills, but we can dispose ourselves to receive his inspirations. This is done by prayer, alms, fasting, the good use of natural resources, particularly of the intelligence. A text of St Bonaventure is particularly relevant here: it concerns the dogma of the procession of the Holy Spirit. This has, he says, its basis in Scripture, and this basis is common to both Greeks and Latins. Theological reasoning elaborates this and it is this level that the Greeks are wrong in wishing to restrict the scriptural statements to the domain of the temporal mission or procession. In doing this they have closed up the way of revelation by which God accomplishss his communication of the texts' meaning. (*In I Sent*, d. 11.)

We have many witnesses to affirm that the understanding of Scripture is a special objectof this *inspiratio* or *revelatio*: St Justin's account of his conversion; St Cyprian's almost exclusive insistence on Scripture as the sole norm; Saints Jerome and Augustine; and other Fathers and medieval doctors. It must suffice here to refer to Gratian's famous remark, in 1140,

on the norms of law: there, the Fathers are called
tractatores, commentators: certain of them excelled
both by a more extensive knowledge and a more
abundant grace of the Holy Spirit, and thus their
commentaries have even, on occasion, enjoyed a
greater authority than those of certain popes.
(Friedberg, 65.)

The result of this divine action is the *understanding*
of the text. The Greek Fathers, in this connection,
spoke of *gnosis*. St Paul asked that his faithful hearers
should be filled with *gnosis*: he himself professed to
have received this gift. By it he meant a rich and
living knowledge of God's plan, the "mystery" of
Christ (cf Eph 3:14–19; Phil 3:8; etc.). Following
St Paul, the Fathers called *gnosis* a spiritual gift which
has for its object or content the knowledge of the
ways of God, the understanding of the great saving
acts accomplished by Christ, and of their proclamation in Scripture.

This spiritual gift of understanding enables us to
enter into the depths of a text. Unanimously, the
Fathers and medieval writers thought that the deeper
meaning of a text was beyond the literal sense,
although only to be reached *through* the literal sense.
And since the method by which one thing is communicated by means of another was called "allegory",
so also the deepest meaning, which one comes to by
the study of the literal meaning, going beyond it
ad interiora, was also known as "allegory". Scripture
was a kind of sacrament with its outer and inner
reality, and the believer was invited to pass from the

first to the second with the aid of God's revelatory action. The very word *sacramentum* was peculiarly fitted to express all this.

4. *The content of this understanding or gnosis is the Christian mystery as the key to the unity of the two Testaments, in whole and in part alike*

To heretics who would only admit what was contained in documentary evidence, that is in the Jewish Scriptures, St Ignatius of Antioch retorted: "My archives are Jesus Christ." This meant that the centre and meaning of every testimony to the work of God is contained in Jesus Christ. Ignatius did not use the word "tradition", but according to St Irenaeus the content of the tradition received by the Church from the apostles is their *kerygma*, that is, the exegesis of the economy, an explanation of Scripture with reference to the Christian mystery of which Scripture speaks fully enough. The same is true, with slight changes of emphasis, for Clement of Alexandria, Origen and St Augustine.

This true meaning of Scripture consists first of all in a christological reading of the Old Testament which allows us to grasp the *consonantia* of the two Testaments. In the New Testament itself, such a reading bestows the perception of its total significance for the Christian life and the Church's life, and for the Christian eschatological hope: in short, the full and detailed content of the covenant relation accomplished in Jesus Christ. Finally, this reading consists, in regard to individual texts, in perceiving the meaning of these texts within the total architecture of "system". The error of the Gnostics, according to St Irenaeus, is to make a selection from Scripture, a text here, and a text there, without reading it within Tradition, that is, with the awareness of its complete meaning, as inherited by the Church from the apostles. (*PG* 7, 521.) This remark of Irenaeus is, alas, equally applicable to present-day sects. On the other hand, when one places oneself in the right perspective, and contemplates Christ, and then, in this light, the true relation established between God and man, all the prophetical writings are clarified and blended together in harmony. As at Cana, tasteless water becomes a full-flavoured, inspiriting wine, the veil is lifted and things that before seemed meaningless take on their meaning.

We are not talking here, in Tradition, of *particular truths* not contained in the scriptural deposit or at least not in that which Scripture bears witness to. St Irenaeus even says that there could be no truths which the apostles did not pass on in a public manner. No; we are talking here of the meaning of the whole. If we can find in "Tradition" particular truths which were not expressed in Scripture, this will doubtless be due to Tradition's own proper genius, by means of the "analogy of faith", in other words, thanks to the light that can be thrown on some particular question by the interrelation of various truths with one another, with their centre and with the end term of the whole investigation. This is peculiarly the case with the two Marian doctrines defined in the modern period, the Immaculate Conception and bodily Assumption of the Mother of God.

Such is, according to the Fathers, the fundamental relationship between Scripture and Tradition. They would have approved of the formula of the contemporary writer who characterized Tradition as "a scriptural instinct consubstantial with Scripture". This was the habitual practice, the grace and special genius of the Fathers. This is also the grace and special genius of the liturgy, and we could illustrate this from the usage—so often clarifying and educative for the Christian understanding of the texts—of Scripture in the Church's annual cycle, or from the means whereby the Church sees and illuminates the Marian mystery through an accumulation of the biblical texts which bear witness to the divine plan.

5. *The "locus" of God's self-revelatory action, and of his communication of the understanding of the Word, is the Church, made up of men who have been converted to Christ.*

The unanimous thought of the Fathers, and of theologians of all times, goes on further to affirm that Scripture can be authentically preserved and its true meaning fully understood only in the Church. St Irenaeus sees the Church as the "place" where the reading of Scripture is authentic, because it is the place of the divine charisms, and these charisms are found in particular among the presbyters, who have the apostolic succession. The same assertion is found in Origen and—we only mention this text, after Franzelin, as witnessing to the common doctrine of the third century—in the pseudo-Clementine *Recognitiones*. "Those who are outside the Church", said St Hilary, "cannot have any understanding of God's Word." (*PL* 9, 933.) "We cannot", continues St Cyril of Jerusalem, "learn and profess the faith except in receiving it as transmitted by the Church, and protected by the texts of holy Scripture." (*PG* 33, 520f.) Commenting on the verse of the psalm: "He has stretched out the heavens like a tent", St Augustine interprets it figuratively, seeing this heaven as Scripture, and he adds: "God has placed this authority first of all in his Church." (*PL* 37, 1341.) For St Augustine, Scripture and the Church are two instances, each with some degree of immediacy incorporating the divine authority. They are interdependent, and the faithful can submit properly to one only in submitting to the other. It is for this reason that we can gather from St Augustine, sometimes texts primarily referring to Scripture and then to the Church, as to an additional authority, and sometimes texts placing the rule of faith in the living consciousness and teaching of the Church. In any case, we must follow Scripture as it has been transmitted to us from the time of Christ and the apostles by a succession of bishops and as it has come down to us, preserved, recommended and explained by the *Catholica*. We have seen already what Vincent of Lerins thought.

This traditional position remains that of the

63

Middle Ages, often also with a more precise insistence on the canonical and institutional structures of the Church. It remains that of modern Catholic theology too. Though Tradition, as far as dogma is concerned, consists principally in the integral interpretation of Scripture from the christological, soteriological, ecclesiological and eschatological viewpoints, this Tradition expresses itself in the teaching of the Church.

This teaching of the Church is the rule of faith. This expression, "rule of faith", refers, in the Fathers, not to a formal regulative principle, but to the concrete rule found in the Church's faith preserved by the succession, which the catechumen accepts and in the profession of which he is baptized. Our faith is concretely conditioned by the structures in which God has conveyed his revelation and which he has given to his covenant. Thus, St Thomas Aquinas, whose astonishing sense of the wholly theological character of the act of faith is almost without parallel in other theologians, could nevertheless define its determining motive in these terms: "The adherence of faith is given to all the articles of faith because of . . . the first Truth as it is proposed to us in Scripture, properly understood according to the Church's teaching." (*ST* II–II, 2.5, a.3, ad 2.)

One must always return to the Church's faith and the Church's teaching, and one starts from these in judging. Where this teaching has not yet been formally expressed, it nevertheless exists in some virtual or latent manner, in the *sensus ecclesiasticus*, the *phronēma ekkēsiastikon* which Eusebius speaks of in citing St Hippolytus, so happy an expression that it was taken up by all the theologians of Tradition in the nineteenth century. Other expressions have approximately the same meaning: that Christian sense, that feeling of the *ecclesia* about the real content of its belief. The New Testament spoke of *dianoia*, the active faculty of understanding (1 Jn 2:20–27; Jn 6:45), and the Latin Fathers of *sensus, intelligentia, intellectus*. We have spoken about this Catholic sense already under it subjective aspect of a spiritual instinct, and its objective aspect as communion or unanimity: both are made active by the influence of the Holy Spirit. We shall return later to the *consensus Patrum*.

The Fathers and the medievals understand by "Church" not only, as we have seen, the whole Christian community, but a fundamentally spiritual reality. It is true that beginning with the Gregorian Reform (last third of the eleventh century) a juridical mode of thought slowly infiltrated into ecclesiological ideas and ended by an invasion of the modern treatises *De Ecclesia*. The rediscovery of Tradition was only made in the nineteenth century with Möhler and the Tübingen school and the influence of this on Passaglia, Franzelin, Scheeben, with Newman also, and then in the twentieth century.

When the Fathers and the medieval writers, not yet influenced by a legalistic view of things, speak of Tradition, whether they use the word or not, as an ecclesial understanding of revelation, of which the canonical Scriptures are, as it were, the real presence, they understand by the "Church" less a hierarchical charism, juridically assured and exercised, than the mystery of the Bride, unceasingly turning from sinfulness to purity, striving to live a life of perfect fidelity towards the Spouse, and of openness to his Spirit. They understand it as the totality of men who are converted to Jesus Christ, and in whom the Spirit is at work. From Origen to St Gregory, including St Augustine, the Fathers inform us that *gnosis* or understanding is given to the souls who are converted to Jesus Christ: "The veil is lifted from the eyes of a Church which has been converted to the Lord," said Origen. (*GCS*, 204f.) "If we do not look to Jesus Christ, the Scriptures become tasteless; if we taste the Saviour there, all is light and understanding, all is reason," says St Augustine, who recalls the change of attitude in the disciples at Emmaus: their doubt and disillusion before their recognition of Christ ("We had hoped . . ."), then the warmith and joyful certainty of their souls when they have recognized him and their hearts are opened: "Were not our hearts burning within us?" (*PL* 35, 1459.) Elsewhere, Augustine writes that when the Church is converted and turns to Christ, the veil is lifted from its eyes and it receives the interior grace of justification. (*PL* 44, 219.) Origen's remarks on the Transfiguration were in the same vein: when Moses bears witness to Christ, the veil which covered his face falls, and his face becomes completely luminous. In the Middle Ages we sometimes find the same idea in the depiction of Christ with one hand crowning the Church, whilst with the other he removes the bandage covering the eyes of the Synagogue: *Quod Moyses velat, Christi doctrina revelat*" ("what was veiled in Moses is now revealed in the teaching of Christ"). This profound idea, according to which we *see* the true meaning of a text when we turn and come to Christ, so as to find him everywhere in it, is at the basis of typological exegesis (or "allegorical" exegesis, in the early meaning of the word); the frequent want of attention to the literal sense in the use of the principle should not be allowed to discredit the principle itself, which is found throughout Tradition, and whose theological value is obvious.

This Church exists principally in spiritual men, or, in the Pauline and Augustine sense of the word, in the saints. *Sancti* is also the title given by the scholastics to the *auctoritates*, that is, to the men who, by a *revelatio* or *inspiratio* from God, had received the gift of understanding or had penetrated the *allegoria* of the sacred text. The use of such a title serves to indicate the preference given to the realities of spiritual anthropology over juridical categories.

The members of the hierarchy themselves, bishops and popes, were in particular considered, in the domain of spiritual knowledge, as spiritual men: for, as they were called to a function instituted by God, they were essentially "charismatics". They were charismatics in a special sense—from their insertion

67

into a Gospel institution endowed with a promise from the Lord ("Where two or three are gathered together in my name . . .")—in the holding of councils: unanimity was the sign of the Holy Spirit's presence. For this reason, the councils were conscious, gathered together, as they were, in the Spirit (which did not prevent them at the same time from being very "historical" and human!) of extending and unfolding the meaning of the revelation attested in Scripture. The councils promulgated "the faith professed by the Fathers according to the Scriptures". (St Athanasius; *PG* 26, 104.)

If spiritual men are thus the bearers of Tradition, this Tradition must itself be holy, *heilige Überlieferung*. That is holy which comes from God, who alone is holy, from his Spirit, who is the *Holy* Spirit. It is because the promptings of this Spirit are at the origin of the whole succession of genuine spiritual gnosis whose total aggregate, stored up and transmitted through the centuries, forms its basis, that we can justly term Tradition itself holy. The consciousness of this sacred character was unhappily obscured in the controversial writings of the sixteenth and seventeenth centuries. This is not yet true of the first anti-Lutheran controversialists, who still had the general formation and spirit of the pre-Tridentine schools, thanks to whom, also, the council itself produced texts of such a rich theological character. Nor is this defect found among those who were nourished on the patristic writings, Bossuet, Thomassin, for instance, but it is seen among the more plodding type of controversialist in the post-Tridentine period. These controversies were carried on in a complete divorce from any sort of spiritual consideration. It is not that spiritual dimensions were unknown to these authors: St Robert Bellarmine wrote works of spirituality, and was not alone in doing so; but it was at this time that theology and spirituality split off from each other into two different realms, with self-sufficient frameworks. Life's spiritual conditions were doubtless presupposed, but they did not enter into the epistemological structure of Tradition. This was seen as a quasi-mechanical transmission of an already constituted deposit. Though intended as a living supplement to lifeless texts, as an interaction of living beings on one another, and ultimately as the action of God in giving life to the believer, it seemed, on the contrary, to have shrunk into a mere series of texts marshalled in support of a juridically authoritative principle drawn from the closely argued conclusions of treatises *De Locis Theologicis*. The *Probatur ex Traditione* of the manuals is usually quite as alien to the historical meaning of the texts and their contexts, as to the theological and Christian meaning of God's continuing action in his Church.

If the Holy Spirit is mentioned in such chapters *De Traditione*, it is in an external way, as the assured guarantee of the Church's infallibility (meaning the infallibility of the hierarchical magisterium whose links with the Christian community are envisaged in a unilateral, juridical manner). There is no refer-

ence now to the necessity for a continuing effort of
conversion to Christ: it seems that the Church no
longer has to strive for full fidelity, no longer has to
strive to call down upon herself the visitation of the
Spirit. Spiritual anthropology now seems to have
been drawn off from ecclesiology; the legal structure
is all-sufficient with its guaranteed administrative
charisms. We have already quoted Möhler's comment
on this matter: "God created the hierarchy and thus
provided more than sufficiently for the needs of the
Church until the end of time." By God's grace, we
are today emerging from the seven years of famine.

6. *The unanimous consensus of the Fathers of the*
Ecclesia *clearly indicates a "locus" of the divine action*
In every age the consensus of the faithful, still more
the agreement of those who are commissioned to
teach them, has been regarded as a guarantee of
truth: not because of some *mystique* of universal
suffrage, but because of the Gospel principle that
unanimity and fellowship in Christian matters
requires, and also indicates, the intervention of the
Holy Spirit. From the time when the patristic
argument first began to be used in dogmatic controversies—it first appeared in the second century and
gained general currency in the fourth—theologians
have tried to establish agreement among qualified
witness of the faith, and have tried to prove from
this agreement that such was in fact the Church's
belief. As a matter of fact, a few testimonies sufficed,
even that of one single man if his particular situation

or the consideration accorded him by the Church were such as to give to what he said the value of coming from a quasi-personification of the whole Church at that time. The decisive factor was not mere quantity but the representative quality of the testimony: *Non numerentur, sed ponderentur*!

Unanimous patristic consent as a reliable *locus theologicus* is classical in Catholic theology; it has often been declared such by the magisterium and its value in scriptural interpretation has been especially stressed (cf. DS 1507, 1863, 2830, 3007; etc.)

Application of the principle is difficult, at least at a certain level. In regard to individual texts of Scripture total patristic consensus is rare. In fact, a complete consensus is unnecessary: quite often, that which is appealed to as sufficient for dogmatic points does not go beyond what is encountered in the interpretation of many texts. But it does sometimes happen that some Fathers understood a passage in a way which does not agree with later Church teaching. One example: the interpretation of Peter's confession in Matthew 16:16–19. Except at Rome, this passage was not applied by the Fathers to the papal primacy; they worked out an exegesis at the level of their own ecclesiological thought, more anthropological and spiritual than juridical.

This instance, selected from a number of similar ones, shows first that the Fathers cannot be isolated from the Church and its life. They are great, but the Church surpasses them in age, as also by the breadth and richness of its experience. It is the Church, not

the Fathers, the consensus of the *Church* in sub-
mission to its Saviour which is the sufficient rule of
our Christianity. This instance shows too that we
may not, at the doctrinal as distinct from the purely
historical level, take the witnesses of Tradition in a
purely material sense: they are to be weighed and
valued. The plain material fact of agreement or dis-
agreement, however extensive, does not allow us to
speak of a *consensus Patrum* at the properly dogmatic
level, for the authors studied in theology are only
"Fathers" in the theological sense if they have in
some way begotten the Church which follows them.
Now, it may be that the seed which will be most
fruitful in the future is not the most clearly so at
present, and that the lifelines of faith may not pass
through the great doctors in a given instance. Historical documentation is at the factual level; it must leave
room for a judgment made not in the light of the
documentary evidence alone, but of the Church's faith.

It can, however, be seen that as regards the
explanation of a *particular* text, or a *particular* article
of doctrine, the theological weight of the *consensus
Patrum* is subject to so many conditions that it
cannot be easily assessed. Students and devotees of
the Fathers—among whom I should wish to number
myself—might well feel disappointed if they had no
other guidance. But, for a start, there are the foundations of faith, the articles on which the whole structure
rests; there are the directions, meanings and spiritual
climate in which the content and implications of our
covenant relation, as attested in Scripture, have been

lived, developed, specified and defended. As far as the reading of Scripture is concerned, there has been built up in that way something more valuable than an interpretative exegetical consensus on some individual verse, I mean the total framework, inside which and starting from which all Catholic reading of written revelation has been formed and educated. This is the most important element, the essential contribution of the Fathers to the formation of an exegetical Tradition.

When we see the Fathers in this way, as those who have formed the milieu of the Church's historical growth, we find that they are unanimous, we are at the heart of their real consensus. We have seen that Tradition is for a Christian almost what the educational milieu is for man in general; the child needs to form its own conclusions in a milieu which provides him with security; it is fundamentally the role of the Fathers to provide such an element in the Church.

7. *The sense in which Tradition represents something distinct from Scripture*

At the risk of one or two repetitions, I wish to elaborate further on the fundamental principle governing the relations between the canonical writings and the Church's Tradition, as outlined in the foregoing paragraphs.

Scripture does not yield its meaning entirely by itself. Text must be complemented by interpretation, as is evidenced by the numerous interpretations to which any one text may be subject. Christians do not read the Old Testament in the same way as the Jews, who would, indeed, refuse the epithet "Old". On the other hand, a Dutch Protestant author remarked recently: "Was not the Reformation's watch-word *Scripture only*? I suggest that the plurality of Churches contradicts this slogan."

We need to go still further: Scripture is not, by itself, the word and message by which God purposes to give life to men. It is, ot be sure, the word of God inasmuch as God has assumed responsibility for it, but of itself it is not God's word in the sense that God could be called the subject of the act of speaking to me. His Word is, in a sense, laid down or deposited; it has become an object, a "thing", in the scriptural text, and by this means what was said once can span the centuries and reach me in the present. But in order that its content may be rendered actual in a living mind, its meaning must be perceived in the present moment by such a mind, as a result of a new act by God: this is no longer the original act by which the sacred writer was inspired, but an act by which God communicates the meaning of his Word to his people, in the fellowship of the prophets and apostles.

The Catholic apologists of the sixteenth century continually taxed the Protestants for identifying Scripture with the Word of God. St Robert Bellarmine observed shrewdly that the disciples journeying to Emmaus knew Hebrew, that the apostles fearfully gathered together in Jerusalem after the crucifixion also knew Hebrew, and that Queen Candace's eunuch could read the text of Isaiah. But what they lacked was *the meaning* of the revelation to which the texts bore witness; Jesus gave this understanding to the apostles, who passed it on to the Church, where it is preserved through the renewing power of the Spirit. Fundamentally, Scripture is only a witness to a revelation that has been made, and a means given by God for the revelation he wishes to make to us of himself and his salvation. This revelation is only fully itself *when it is made to someone*, when it is *actually received by a living mind* in the act of faith which demands an action, in us, of the living God bearing witness to himself: "He who believes in the Son of God has the testimony in himself" (1 Jn 5:10.) The living theology of the Middle Ages had a clear realization of this. It is the basis of the thoroughly theological doctrine of St Thomas on the act of faith. There were, it was held, two stages in God's self-revelation: the act which he posited once and for all in the *ephapax* of the prophets, Christ, and the apostles; and the action which he promised to accomplish continually in the Church throughout the ages.

The first stage of God's self-revelatory action was the definitive formation of an objective deposit; the second, the Gospel's flowering in a personal human subject, throughout an endlessly varied history. Scripture is what was posited once and for all, the Word of God as completed. The Church's Tradition, conceived not just as a material object but as the active presence of revelation in a living subject, by

75

the power of the Holy Spirit, represents what is as yet unfulfilled, in progress, ceaselessly requiring fulfilment, in the Word of God. Here Protestantism fears lest the progressive element should oust the original deposit completely, lest it tend to become innovation, creation, and the Church itself virtually independent of the Word. Here we touch the most crucial and delicate point in the question of the relations between Scripture and Tradition. It is no solution to sacrifice either of these terms to the other. It always seems to Protestants that we sacrifice Scripture, whereas they generally seem to us to sacrifice the Church. It is not that they are unaware of the need for some divine act other than the original scriptural inspiration given unrepeatably to the prophets and apostles: the doctrine of the Spirit's inner witness, indeed, insists on the necessity of another activity, at the present moment, *in ourselves*. But this present activity is seen (1) as strictly limited to the elucidation of *Scripture* (Why?); and (2) within the framework of individual understandings, not of the Church as such.

The twofold aspect of God's revelatory activity corresponds to the duality in the missions of Christ and the Holy Spirit. Christ is the "form" of grace and truth given once and for all time; the Spirit is the power granted to persons who multiply and succeed one another throughout human history. The Spirit is truly the Spirit *of Christ*, as promised and sent by Christ to recall, deepen, make clear, and apply everything that Christ said (Jn 14:26; 16:13–15).

But it is also true that the Spirit is given to the Church, and to each believer within the Church's unity and according to the place which is his in the whole body of Christians.

Some kind of development is necessarily entailed: at least, as an unfolding or an explanation. The Church is commissioned to proclaim and to fulfil the plan of the covenant established in Jesus Christ in an earthly context. The Church is both transmission and life, both repetition and reissuing, a response given on the basis of the one and only text to the ever new questions asked by time. It is the making present in personal and world history of the saving plan made in Jesus Christ, and it requires a future fulfilment. The Holy Spirit bears witness to the Church, that what it preaches is indeed the content of the mission it received to proclaim the Gospel. He enlightens the Church about the true content of the economy of salvation and this activity cannot thwart in any way what God has already done in speaking by his servants the prophets, in the written testimony of revelation, but at the same time, it is not reducible to a written testimony. It depends, in point of fact, on the work of God, which is certainly not reducible to scriptural inspiration, and which is at work in Tradition.

Recent Catholic theology has dwelt insistently on this aspect of Tradition, especially in connexion with modern development in Marian dogma. We have not disguised the danger, in this matter, of admitting a kind of autonomous life in Tradition, in regard to the original deposit, and especially the scriptural witness. If the magisterium elucidates Scripture, it first and always submits itself to Scripture and must be ready to receive from it. We could not grant to it a virtual autonomy, against which, moreover, its own most solemn declarations protest. But Protestants, calling attention to such declarations, add that the Church's present practice appears to them out of harmony with such a rule. They hold that in practice living Tradition is equiparated to a new revelation, although the Holy Spirit's activity is stated to be guaranteed only for the conservation and the faithful explanation of the unique revelation made once and for all. (Cf. Vatican I; DS 3069.)

Doubtless the debate will only be concluded when the Spirit has aided out separated brethren to understand that which the Church believes he has in fact enabled her to understand. We ourselves can only take care that no "development" should occur or become established which cannot be justified, *within the living Tradition*, on the basis of the revealed deposit, and we must apply ourselves to showing our separated brethren by what stages, against the background of the analogy of faith, the relevant articles have commended themselves to our Christian fidelity as belonging to the economy attested to by Scripture, and lived out by the Church under the action of the Holy Spirit.

3. Liturgy, Principal Instrument of the Church's Tradition

"It is through the liturgy . . . that 'the work of our redemption is exercised'. The liturgy is thus the chief means by which the faithful can express in their lives, and manifest to others, the mystery of Christ and the real nature of the true Church."—*Constitution on the Sacred Liturgy*, Introduction, 2.

I want these few pages to be a hymn of filial homage and respect. There will be no details of a juridical sort on the conditions under which some particular text, or the existence of a feast, may or may not be cited as proof for a theological assertion. We are here concerned with the liturgy as the expression of a Church actively living, praising God, and bringing about a holy communion with him: the covenant as fulfilled in Christ Jesus, its Lord, Head, and Spouse. *Vox Populi (Dei)*, *vox Corporis (Christi)*, *vox Sponsae*! Not the voice of the magisterium teaching, defining, reproving, condemning, or refuting, but the voice of the loving, praying Church, doing more than merely expressing its faith: hymning it, practising it, in a living celebration, wherein too, it makes a complete self-giving. For this reason, the liturgy is assured of a character and a place without parallel as an instrument of tradition, as much because of its style or characteristic forms, as because of its content.

Value as an educative milieu

The liturgy is a privileged custodian and dispenser of Tradition, for it is by far the principal and primary thing among all the actions of the Church. It is, indeed, the active celebration of the Christian mystery, and as it celebrates and contains the mystery in its fulness, it transmits all the essential elements of this mystery.

That the liturgy is a *locus theologicus* of a special kind is too well known to be in need of proof. This is due to the very nature of the liturgy, which is worship and consequently has the character of a witnessing to or a profession of faith. Even if we take the well-known saying *Lex orandi, lex credendi* in its original sense admitted by Pius VII, it is still true that the Church has invested the whole of its faith in its prayer, and though fervour does not *create* truth, yet the liturgy contains, offers, and expresses in its own way all of the mysteries, only certain aspects of which have been formulated by our theological understanding and in dogmas. "The Church did not begin by saying that bread was being changed into Christ's Body and that wine was being changed into Christ's Blood; what it began by saying and still says, is: 'This is my Body, this is my Blood'; the additional concept of change may almost be called an afterthought." (Vorsier).

Recent writers have laid stress on the fact that liturgical worship, and especially the sacraments, are a channel through which the revelation of God's saving plan in Jesus Christ comes to us; the liturgy bears witness to the mysteries, it proclaims them in its celebration of them, continually presenting to us the most fundamental scriptural truths, while enabling us to make a fitting response of welcome and praise to the Word which it proclaims. This aspect of worship should be acceptable to Protestants, especially to those of the Calvinist tradition who define a sacrament as *verbum visibile*, and attribute to it an essentially cognitive value. In this way, they tend to stress the pulpit at the expense of the altar; and this has often been reflected in their church architecture.

Altar and pulpit both have their distinct places in the communication of salvation in the Church. Tradition is preserved and communicated by both of them. The pulpit—the written and spoken word—communicates knowledge by means of conceptual signs and formulas; the altar communicates the very substance of the reality, in signs which contain it or produce its fruits. This is what differentiates sacramental communion from a simply spiritual communion, whose efficacy depends entirely on the dispositions of the believer. With reference to St Ignatius of Antioch's famous "The faith which is the Lord's flesh, and the *agapé* which is the blood of Jesus Christ", Fr Nautin writes that "The apostles' Tradition is no mere intellectual thing, but a sacramental deposit, the *pistis* of baptism, with its completion in *agapé*, the Eucharist". In a sacrament more is received, and transmitted, than could be expressed or grasped; that is why, though realizing the great value of feasts and celebrations for teaching the truth, above all to those of simple faith, we must avoid "using" the liturgical actions

and sacramentals overmuch for the instruction of
the faithful or the semi-pagan who are attracted to
these ceremonies, stifling the liturgy with learned
doctrinal explanations, or even treating it as an
occasion for proselytizing. The liturgy's own way of
teaching in its confession of faith, or in the profession
of faith it makes in its act of praise (the doxologies
are of great theological value) is not the style a
teacher, or even a theologian, would use: the liturgy
simply goes ahead, calmly confident, with the affirmation of what it does and affirming the content of what
it hands on in its celebration. This, too, is the way
in which Tradition works, communicating the conditions for life just as it communicates that life itself.
All this has been expressed in typically brilliant and
biting prose, with a polemical edge to it, by Joseph
de Maistre:

> The creeds which later appeared [after the time of
> the apostles] are professions of faith by which
> Christians might know one another or oppose the
> errors of a particular time. In them you may read:
> *We believe*, but never: *You shall believe*. We recite
> them in private; we sing them in our places of
> worship, with strings and organ (Ps 150:4), as true
> prayers, because they are formulas of submission,
> confidence and faith addressed to God, and not
> ordinances addressed to me. I should rather like
> to see musical settings of the *Augsburg Confession*
> and the *Thirty-Nine Articles*: it would be very
> amusing!

Newman has said as much, in his own quietly eirenic and lucid manner, in a letter of 1837 to his sister:

I doubt whether one should look to the service for the *doctrine* of the Church about Confirmation, though it *might* be there. Prayers are not sermons, except accidentally. The Puritans, &c., wished so to make them; they looked upon sacraments chiefly *as* sermons, and thought their grace *lay* in their kindling impressions in the mind; hence they generally started with a long preachment: in the extreme Protestant (Continental) baptismal services, that is, you have a long exhortation. In the same spirit Bucer, in King Edward's Second Book, prefixed the Exhortation at the beginning of the daily service, which still forms part of the service: in the primitive way, the worshipper did not think of himself—he came to God—God's house and altar were the sermon which addressed him and roused him. His Sacraments were *the objects* of his regards. Words were unnecessary.

Hence in Ordination the laying on of hands is the whole. There are no words necessary. . . . Hence in our Confirmation service the Exhortation is an address to those who come, demanding of them what *they have to give*. They give their *word*. The bishop imposes his hand—such is the interchange. The *action* speaks; it must be a gift. What else is meant by *laying hands* on?

I conceive this is plain to common-sense, even, if the bishop said not a word in administering the rite.

Newman's example is a very striking one. Every priest has lived it out many times in his life. It is true that the ordination liturgy explains the content of the sacrament, as it goes along, but at the precise moment when the priesthood is conferred this is done without words, and yet no one fails to understand the meaning of this silent gesture. At the time of the discussion on Anglican orders, the Anglicans cited in their favour ancient ordination rituals which were no more explicit than Cranmer's. This would not suffice to settle the question, since complete silence will suffice only on condition that it is given meaning by the Church's faith and tradition. In the case of Anglican orders, it is precisely this faith that is in question.

From the liturgy's character as a repository of Tradition and a means of its communication there derive a certain number of marks which make it into a sacred *didascalia*, a tuition in the life of holiness, a kind of spiritual matrix in which Christians are formed.

(i) If we seek precision in the use of concepts, the liturgy can be relatively misleading. Such is my own oft repeated experience: having so many times been overwhelmed with an understanding of the mysteries through an attentive celebration of the liturgy, to which I must admit that I owe at least half of what I have understood in theology, I have many times made (either directly, or by means of some publication) a study of the doctrine contained in the liturgical texts. I have noticed that their marvellously rich content, so continually and inexhaustibly nourishing, does not when studied yield up the expected precise data for theology.

(ii) Again, there is the fact that the liturgy gives the whole thing, in bulk, handing on the mystery of salvation in much the same way as the earliest Christian art, which in one way or another basically always portrays salvation. Thence derives its serene and joyful character. While our dogmas were often formulated against heresies, the liturgy is directed against no one, even though there are a number of collects which have Pelagianism in view, and the *Gloria Patri* is anti-Arian in origin. In the liturgy, as in the patristic writings, because the essential Gospel kerygma is expressed in them we find there is a kind of presence of the whole mystery in every part, which gives to ever part its meaning, as a centre gives meaning to what surrounds it. Now, as we shall see better in a later chapter, the *meaning* of things is Tradition's most precious contribution. In a pre-eminent way, Tradition shares and gives catholicity. Within Tradition, since it is continually at the centre, everything is given *in toto*, communicating its full presence and power.

(iii) The liturgy's *didascalia* has a sacred character which we should like to describe as "mysteric", with reference to Odo Casel. Scripture is the work of the Spirit, accomplished through men filled with the Spirit. The liturgy, communicating salvation in abstraction from the written word, must use special and sacred means: the sacraments, spiritual men, and the consecrated community. We may recall the liturgical and monastic atmosphere in which teaching was carried on in the Church before the rise of scholasticism. *Sacra Pagina, Scientia sacra, Sacra Doctrina, Divina Traditio.* In the liturgy we find a holy thing and its celebration, a holy thing that presupposes a basis of prayer, fasting and openness to the Spirit. Tradition itself bears witness to this, creating its own conditions for existence, as a rule for the life of a holy Church, whose ideal form, perhaps, would be a little bit monastic, rather than a Church given up to completely external, secular rules of life, whose decisions are made only in departmental offices, and are measurable only by a geometrical, juridical ideal. We may add that one cannot be too wary, in this respect, of the great harm that may well have been done by a collection of texts like that of Denzinger, despite its great fame and genuine usefulness.

(iv) Let us add, too, that the liturgy is by nature conservative. Its essence is the preservation intact of something entrusted to the faithful and withdrawn from profanation. By its nature, too, it is both congregational and hierarchical, the act of a whole people as well as of men specially ordained. It thus shows, in a specially notable way, the pattern that, as we have already seen, belongs to a *subject* of Tradition.

Style or manner

Everything turns on the fact that the liturgy is not just theoretical or notional statement, but sacred *action.* This action or activity is synthetic, incorporating and expressing a conviction, and at the same time developing it and conveying it to others. The liturgy is not a manual, working with clear concepts and definitions: it procures entry into the Christian truths by way of prayer and actions, by familiar signs expressing men's faithfulness and love. The entry into these truths is not by way of discussion or argument, but through the intimacy of living experience. "We need to feed slowly upon things themselves, rather than upon the explanations of things." (Duplogé.) For the Church, the liturgy is not a dead monument, a kind of Pantheon to be visited as one visits a museum, but a home which is always lived in, the conditioning envelope or atmosphere of its whole life.

Nevertheless, as a ritualized activity, the liturgy has a monument's powers of conservation. Ritual is a fixed thing, transmitted and performed in a fixed manner. On the one hand, there is the risk of empty formalism, "tradition" in the sense of mechanical, routine gesture: we know this only too well! But on the other hand, there are splendid resources here for tradition in its broad sense of fidelity and fullness. Ritual preserves: while everything changes, and we ourselves pass through phases which are not always those of continuous growth, ritual remains. The fourteenth and fifteenth centuries come, with their loss of all liturgical feeling, and their exaggerations and excrescences in the shape of human demonstrative and tragic devotions of every sort; the eighteenth

89

century, with its taste for the rational and the useful, its distrust of mysterty then the nineteenth century, with its historcism, its critical analyses and destructions. After all this, what has become of the Mass, Easter, the episcopate, anything apart from the Madonnas, the worship of the Supreme Being, or the "Historical Jesus?" How do we fare in the twentieth century, living after so much demolition work? But we need only step into an old church, taking holy water, as Pascal and Serapion did before us, in order to follow a Latin Mass which has scarcely changed since St Gregory the Great, or we may open our missals at the pages which give the Paschal Triduum . . . . Everything has been preserved for us, and we can enter into a heritage which we may easily transmit in our turn, to those coming after us. Ritual, as a means of communication and of victory over devouring time, is also seen to be a powerful means for communion in the same reality between men separated by centuries of change and affected by very different influences.

Both as a lived action and as a ritualized action, the liturgy preserves and hands on to us e lements which are much more numerous than were realized by those men who performed and preserved the rites, and actually handed them on to us: many more, even, than we ourselves can know. The whole Eucharist is given to me in its celebration, I myself possess it in its entirety, although I understand and could express so little of it. The liturgical action is synthetic, its gestures sum up and recapitulate past experience. The whole of our love is expressed in the liturgical kiss, even if we do not really attend sufficiently to what we are doing. The whole of our faith is in the most ordinary sign of the cross, and when we say "Our Father" we already imply all the knowledge which will be given to us only when we embrace it in the revelation of glory.

It is right that we should have re-established the historical meaning of the famous axiom *Legem credendi statuit lex orandi*: the *lex orandi* is not the liturgy but the evangelical and apostolic precept of praying without ceasing and for all necessities; this entails a belief in the necessity also of grace, which is the *lex credendi*. Nevertheless, it is true that we can get to know what we are to believe by starting from an order on how to act, but this advantage is something much greater than a mere dogmatic precision; it contains a more interior element. We come to understand many things through prayer and as a result of prayer: such is the case, for example, with God's attributes, by which we invoke him and in doing so enter into a communion with him. A large part of the Church's belief has become known to it through the holy living-out of its faith, hope and love. Thus the liturgy is the privileged *locus* of Tradition, not only from the point of view of conservation and preservation, but also from that of progress and development. The part it plays in the progressive development of our dogmatic understanding of revelation is considerable. Moreover, it is clear that such growth and development must be controlled by a magisterium which makes constant reference to the objective standards of the apostolic kerygma and especially, for verification, to the scriptural witness.

Content

The liturgy is a celebration, the active recalling or efficacious representation, at the present moment of human and cosmic history, of the mysteries of salvation which were revealed in history at an earlier time. Therefore, it is at one and the same time theology, soteriology, anthropology and cosmism. The liturgy follows the natural time of the world, the rhythm of seasons, weeks, days and hours; it follows the course of human life which, whether on the small day-to-day scale or in a larger way, must unfold in the framework of this rhythm. Into this framework it inserts the fact of Christ, making him present there so that he may become the source of salvation and holiness for men and for the world, and the source of glory for God. It does not insert Christ's work merely by proclamation and teaching but, through the unique and *sui generis* reality of the sacramental order, it is able to assume the form of a present reality, at once hidden and revealed, and active, though never automatically so. Like the Word, which it includes and takes up, the liturgy is the means by which Christ, who dwells in it and acts in it as Priest, King and Prophet, perfects and completes in mankind that new creation which he instituted in his sacred *transitus*. The liturgy has, thus, in another manner the same content as Scripture. Its manner or mode is not narrative and historical, as is Scripture's, retailing a whole series of facts; it centres more upon the mysteries of salvation and upon Christ as fulfilling in his *transitus,* by which he became the cause of ours too, the truth of mankind's covenant relationship with God. The whole of the Bible is paschal, but the liturgy must be so to a greater degree because it is something created in the light of Easter and Pentecost, as illuminated by these events: equally, because it is an active sharing in the *transitus* and not merely its retelling or proclamation. For content it has, in a more concentrated way then Scripture, the truth of the divine-human covenant relationship, finally confirmed in the death and resurrection of Jesus Christ, the unique meeting-point between God and man.

It celebrates this relationship, shares it and gives it life in a biblical, christological and catholic manner. It hands it on to successive generations in its full reality and it is on this account that it is "the principal instrument of the Church's tradition". (Bossuet.) We must explain briefly each of these terms.

The biblical aspect

It is evident to anyone who is acquainted with Scripture and the liturgy that the latter is woven out of scriptural texts and allusions. Many liturgical gestures simply reproduce those mentioned in the Bible. Further, the liturgy's *ethos* is in continuity with that of Scripture. "In both Bible and liturgy

there is one vision of the world, one attitude towards
God and one interpretation of history, to such an
extent that there can be no liturgical life without
some initiation into Scripture, and conversely, the
Bible finds in the liturgy a living commentary which
gives it its fullest meaning." (Martimort.) This living
commentary places the texts in relation to one
another and to their centre, Christ in his paschal
mystery. The marvellous manner in which the liturgy
links texts together, quotes passages, or alludes to
episodes which we should not have thought of ourselves but which, in their new contexts, take on
deeper meanings, is something we must discover for
ourselves, possibly with the help of learned studies.
The liturgy is itself completely centered upon the
paschal mystery, which is its heart precisely because
the Eucharist is its heart. When it celebrates the
Eucharist it celebrates too the Passover, so that it
reads the Scriptures in the same light as that in
which Christ explained them to his followers on ths
way to Emmaus or in Jerusalem on Easter Day
(Lk 23:27, 44-5). Wherever in the world the Eucharist
is celebrated, the liturgy's spiritual location is the
Jerusalem of Easter: it is, as it were, the permanent
making present of that temporal situation.

At one and the same time, following the bent of
Scripture and conforming to its requirements, the
liturgy applies to man in his daily life the reality of
Christ which it makes known, celebrates and shares.
It does this first of all in its texts and prayers. It
does this, too, in the preaching which is *an integral*

part of the liturgical action. The liturgy demands such a commentary, for by it the priesthood, which is essentially a prophetic rather than simply a ritual one, as having the Gospel as its point of origin, teaches men of faith how "today the Scripture you have heard is fulfilled".

The christological aspect

This communication occurs in the same process as a thorough biblical revivifying, and that explains why each liturgical renewal is accompanied by a refocussing of faith on Christ as the centre.

The catholic aspects

We could as well say "Christian", in order to indicate that Christians are always included in what the liturgy proclaims, celebrates, and fulfils. It is not enough for the liturgy to recall the biblical statements together with the events of sacred history: these must find their fulfilment in the hearts of men. Therefore the liturgy is the place where the Christian is never separated from Christ: not only in the sense that without Christ there can be no Christians—a point which protestant biblical studies bring out very well—but in the sense, less stressed by these studies, that without *Christians* Christ would not be present. The biblical character of such a truth is indisputable, but we owe much to the Fathers for recognizing it and asserting it so forcefully. It is continually borne out, also, but the liturgy which shows forth Christ in the act of joining to himself a holy and faithful people; it adds the saints' and its own commentaries to the Word of God himself and celebrates with Christ the mystery of the saints and the communion of saints. The sanctoral cycle and the cult of relics and images possess this meaning, and we must now allow distortions and misplaced emphases to obscure their very real depth and genuineness. On fragments of a vase found among the ruins of a basilica at Belezma in Numidia, which had once contained relics, it is possible to make out the inscription: *In isto vaso sancto congregabuntur membra Christi* ("in this sacred vessel are gathered together the members of Christ"). The liturgy has understood, and will help us too to realize, that if the whole of Scripture unfolds before us man's true relation with God, it does not speak only about Christ, but about us as well, it does not sunder Jesus Christ from his saints: in it he appears as *clothed* with them, as with his visible body.

Among the saints, but linked to Christ's mystery by ties which are not only more close but in fact quite unique, the liturgy celebrates in a very special way "holy Mary, Mother of God". It places her in a relation to the whole plan of God and to the inspired texts by which that plan is communicated to us, and experiencing the Marian mystery in the fact of its celebration, in a way which words are unable to express adequately, the liturgy has stored up an understanding of this mystery which is irreducible to the understanding obtainable by theological study and investigation, no matter how great—but also how precarious—this grasp of the mystery may be. The manner in which the Catholic liturgy, both in the East and the West, using the analogy of faith, applies to Mary themes, images and texts taken from the whole body of Scripture, and especially its most mysterious sections, counts as the most important aspect of Tradition in regard to mariological doctrine. All this is only possible because Mary, as the mother of Jesus, is together with him at the centre of God's saving plan: she is thus seen in a christological light and at the same time as the centre of the mystery of the Church, which is itself at the heart of the redeemed world. But here Tradition extends Scripture while it uses it, reading it with eyes able to perceive a deeper reality than is attainable by purely philological or historical perceptions.

The liturgy communicates our relation to God in its fullness

I have pointed out already that it is the special property of action, as also of symbols and rites, to embody the whole of a reality in a more complete way than the mind can grasp, even confusedly. Likewise, it is the prerogative of the faithful carrying out of the Church's worship to be able to retain and pass on again its heritage, in its entirety, no matter how fragmentary may be our awareness of its actual content. This is true in a quite special way of the liturgical life, and this fact would account for an experience I have had in the ecumenical movement: the study of formularies of belief and dogmatic

D

treatises is not enough if we are to penetrate the full reality of a Christian communion, or even its actual and living belief; we must add to this a concrete knowledge, and hence some sort of experience, of its life and liturgy. You cannot properly understand another Christian until you have seen him at prayer in his own community, and—with all due respect to the laws forbidding *communicatio in sacris*—attended his place of worship to pray with him.

Made up as it is of both action and ritual, the liturgy is in the highest degree synthetic. As is milk for the newly born child, it is a complete food, answering to all requirements and at the same time easily assimilated. It joins up, reconciles and resolves in a higher synthesis, elements which are not only different but even opposed to one another. To show in detail how this occurs would take up too much space and would also take us out of our way, but here is a short-list of the elements:

the universe, man, and God's saving acts; cosmic time and salvation history, retelling of historical facts and dogmatic affirmations;

mystery and symbol, the supra-rational of mystery, the infrarational of symbol;

ordained priesthood and the faithful, fully sacerdotal people of God;

doctrine and action, word and sacrament;

body and soul;

freedom of the spirit and fixed formulas; inspiration and discipline;

the secret and the public; person and community;
God's initiative and man's response or commitment;
simplicity and richness; nature and culture.

Through the liturgy's quite special character, a mass
of questions are resolved in a sane, Christian manner
sometimes before they are even put, or at least
without their being accompanied by tensions and
difficulties: perhaps somewhat like the peaceful solv-
ing, within the calm of a normal family circle, of
questions full of discrepancies and conflicts, for
example, authority and freedom, person and community, continuity and innovation, tension and relax-
ation, etc. It is the liturgy which gives to the Church
the fullness of its family atmosphere; in this it rejoins
Tradition, which is, as we have already seen, something very similar to what education is in the succession, the solidarity and the renewal of the generations.

Because of all this, *the liturgy is "the principal of
the Church's Tradition"*. "It is in the liturgy that the
Spirit who inspired the Scriptures still speaks to us;
the liturgy is tradition itself, at its highest degree of
power and solemnity." (Guéranger.) The liturgy acts
according to the general manner of Tradition, and
since it is endowed with the genius of Tradition, it fills
Tradition's role in a superlative way. Speaking about
the liturgy, and describing its activity, I have felt
myself to be speaking of Tradition itself and describing *its* work. Thus Pius VII could call it "the faithful
mirror of the teaching handed on by our forefathers".

99

4. The Council as an Assembly and the Church as essentially Conciliar

"Just as, by the Lord's will, St Peter and the other apostles constituted a single apostolic college, in a similar way the Roman Pontiff, as the successor of Peter, and the bishops, as the successors of the apostles, are joined together. The collegial nature and meaning of the episcopal order found expression . . . in the conciliar assemblies which made common judgments about more serious matters in decisions reflecting the views of a larger number. The ecumenical councils held through the centuries represent a clear witness to this collegial aspect."—*Dogmatic Constitution on the Church*, III, 23.

There is no lack of treatises on councils. In Catholic theology, however, they seem to be linked either to the anti-conciliarist reaction which persisted up until the middle of the nineteenth century, or, after the First Vatican Council and the trend which prepared it, to the extreme papalism which finally triumphed over the remaining traces of gallicanism; in this context, for example, we find the theses of Passaglia, recently edited by Mgr H. Schauf, or the two chapters by P. D. Palmieri in his *Tractatus de Romano Pontifice cum Prolegomeno de Ecclesia* (Prato, 1891²), who in fact seems to have been acquainted, directly or indirectly, with the teaching of Passaglia. In the case of both these authors the treatise *De Conciliis* is appended to the treatise on the Roman pontiff, which is taken up almost exclusively with a consideration of the Church's magisterium; Palmieri's treatise formulates his theses within the framework of the petrine and papal monarchy, which he takes for granted and considers beyond debate, without even raising the question of the collegial nature, albeit structured organically, of the supreme power in the

Church, stemming from, and in the image of, that of the apostles. What is more, both these writers consider the councils from a purely juridical point of view—but this is a characteristic common to the majority of the ecclesiological treatises of that period; the only questions posed are those of authority and power, of validity and law, and none that are really *theo*logical—the Holy Spirit is not even mentioned! Like most of the classic treatises *De Ecclesia* of that time they are merely documents of public ecclesiastical law.

Even within these limitations, however, much could be said, particularly about the *historical* treatment of texts and facts, but this falls outside the scope of the present paper. Referring not only to tradition and to theology. but also to the conciliar experience which I was privileged to undergo, I should like to touch upon the two following questions, both concerned with the essential nature of councils:

(1) Is the coming together—the assembly as such— necessary for a council?
(2) Secondarily, of what nature is the presence of the Holy Spirit which is guaranteed at a council and inherent in it?

1. *The necessity of assembly*

It doesn't seem serious to ask whether the fact of coming together in one place and actually forming an assembly is truly of the essence of a council. In fact, all the definitions describe a council as *an assembly*. The fathers use expressions which all convey the idea of coming to assemble in one place. This question may be asked, however, and in fact it has been. "A council held by correspondence" has been mentioned with regard to the consultation of the entire Catholic episcopacy by Pius IX, in his encyclical of 2 February 1849, *Ubi primum*, to discover whether the doctrine of the Immaculate Conception of the mother of God could be defined as belonging to the deposit of the Catholic faith, according to the pastors thus called upon to express their personal opinion and that of their flock. This expression was again used in connection with a similar consultation made by Pius XII, in his letter of 1 May 1946, *Deiparae Virginis*, when he wished to define the dogma of the Assumption of the blessed virgin Mary. (*AAS* XLII [1950], 783.) This mention of a kind of council was not entirely irrelevant in the sense that the consultation by the pope was an authentic form of the exercise of the Church's essential collegiality, and therefore of the conciliar nature of its life. Before they were able to meet, at least in any substantial numbers, the bishops would often consult each other by letter, and this was a way of exercising the collegiality of the *episkopé* and of reaching unanimity among themselves. Let us take, as one example among many, this text by Alexander, Bishop of Alexandria, communicating the decisions of the Council of Alexandria which condemned Arius "to all his colleagues, in every part of the catholic church":

As the Catholic Church is composed of a single body, and as the Holy Scriptures tell us to preserve our links of unanimity and peace, we are in the habit of writing to each other to keep ourselves mutually informed of our affairs, so that if one member is suffering or rejoicing we too may suffer or rejoice with the others. [*PG* 67, 44.]

It was not possible, however, to confuse a consultation by correspondence with a council, and alert theologians were not slow in pointing this out: "This vast consultation of the episcopate has been described as a sort of council by correspondence. It is something different, since the bishops were not called upon to take part in the solemn exercise of the extraordinary magisterium, as they do in a council." (M. Labourdette and M. J. Nicolas.) The pope had collected the opinions of the bishops as *teses fidei*, but he promulgated the dogma in his own name, by virtue of his sole authority as head of the Church, the bishops merely playing the role of informants or counsellors.

In a council they are something more than this; they are truly *judices fidei* (cf. DS 3000): they decide, define, and—united to their head or leader—impose a law on the universal church (if the council is ecumenical or general) or on a part of the church (if the council is restricted—i.e., provincial, national, or continental). A single decision, a unique act of judgment, is made by a large number of pastors, forming a single principle of thought and judgment; the subject who acts is the body or college of bishops as such, in which the Bishop of Rome, as Peter's successor, is in the position of *caput*, as well as possessing a personal privilege of infallibility, which is his alone.

Body and *college* are taken synonymously here, as they are so often in the ancient writers: "Company, community, college, body, all these signify more or less the same", wrote Jean d'André. We may note, however, that Hostiensis preferred to restrict the title *collegium* to a collectivity of people *living together*. We know that, at least since St Cyprian, the expression *collegium* was applied to the episcopate: to the totality of bishops scattered in their provinces, as well as those who might be gathered together locally. The college is a gathering of persons who share a single function but who carry it out individually. These persons can come together in order to carry out a single act, which is an act of their college as such, and of each of them as members of the college. This is what happens in a council.

But one could put forward the hypothesis of a collegial act performed without a coming together or assembly in one place. If, for example, Pius IX or Pius XII had considered that affirmative replies to their consultations of 1849 and 1946 expressed the moral unanimity of the Catholic episcopate, and instead of regarding them as simply informative or advisory had regarded them as expressing a true judgment, and had then promulgated the dogmas not in their own name but *in the name of the college*, the dogmatic declaration would have been a collegial act; it could then be debated whether this was not equivalent to a conciliar act, or even formally such an act. This hypothesis was formulated by D. Palmieri, and he answered the question in the affirmative:

> It is clear that this collecting together of the actions of all into one action, this collecting together of opinions and votes, can be achieved by the bishops remaining in their own sees, in which case it may—in its formal aspect at, least—certainly be considered as equivalent to a council. [*Tractatus*, II, 670.]

However, Palmieri went on to add:

> Nevertheless, such a collecting together can normally be achieved more fully and more effectively if the bishops come together to exchange opinions with each other and to vote in each other's presence.

This addition is important and true, and I shall be returning to it as it does not go far enough. I shall attempt to discover, from different points of view and at different levels, the positive and unique contribution of the actual coming together of the members of the college.

1. First, *from a human point of view*—or psychological, if you prefer, but in the case of a council it is the human aspect, the setting and condition of a religious and even supernatural reality—in the

hypothesis of the "council by correspondence", each prelate would be at his desk, isolated, unable to exchange views with or receive help from the others. And, however one explains the origin of councils, it is certain that they fulfil a need, on the one hand of solidarity and communion, and on the other of mutual enrichment and help. It is impossible to reach a true assessment of what needs to be done, alone; and one has no right to claim this, if only in practice, since the Church is a communion, and since anything that is decided in one particular place is of interest, to a certain degree, to all the others. A plenitude is reached through the contributions of others and the exchange of ideas and experiences, which could never result from solitary reflection. Palmieri himself remarks upon this. (*Tractatus*, ii, 693.) And this is something more than a mere question of information, which could be supplied by writing. The assembly as such provides a milieu, and also the conditions for the formation of a living conviction.

A milieu is a context which somehow unites the exteriority of the objective with the immanence of life; we live in a milieu, and yet it penetrates us, it is within us, and this is what differentiates it from a simple "place". In this way the precarious and weak aspects of our attitudes are strengthened by the presence of others. Indeed, in their presence we are encouraged and even impelled to express ourselves and our commitment to the full. We have all experienced this fact, as also the kind of exaltation and expansion that comes from participating in a large meeting. One is lifted out of oneself, as it were, enriched, elevated and enlarged by what one has heard and received from the others. As St John Chrysostom said, "Just as steel sharpens steel, so a meeting increases charity"; it also increases determination, understanding, and a spirit of enterprise. Aren't these the very things that the bishops witness to having experienced at the Vatican Council?

A written consultation can be a form of dialogue, but it never has the same effect as the living exchange of an encounter, during which one's thought is formed and modified—sometimes by a single word or suggestion; sometimes by the impact of a powerful conviction.

In a council it is either a question of clarifying the tradition of the Church or the *sensus ecclesiae*, or of producing a solution to a contemporary question. Both the *sensus ecclesiae* and the desired solution lie hidden in the memory or consciousness of the Church—or rather, in the memories and consciousness of the persons who compose the Church. These memories and consciousnesses must communicate in order to produce a common expression and sum total, so to speak, of the memory and consciousness of the Church. This is not a collection of personal convictions, for although it only exists personified in actual men—and, at the highest level, in the consciousness of Christ and in his Spirit, but I shall speak of this later—it nonetheless transcends these men and through them belongs to the Church. The council aims at achieving a totalization of the memory of the Church, by a communication of the consciences which house this memory. Can this be done by means of a written consultation? It is possible, but only up to a certain point. This communication of consciousness necessary to realize and express their communion presupposes an exchange which is only perfect in a direct contact, and this explains the calling of an assembly. The "council by writing" would allow a collegial act to be arrived at, that would possess the same *juridical* value as a conciliar decision; but in fact an act by the pope alone would have the same value, juridically speaking! In such a "council by writing" there would be no conciliar procedure, and therefore no authentic conciliar act either. The plentitude would be lacking that the most papalist of theologians assert to be the prerogative of the consiliar action in comparison with the infallible act of the pope himself, when acting alone.

2. *The juridical point of view* is concerned with the external conditions of validity and with the degree of coercion or obligation; it ignores the internal or moral conditions and the intimate nature of things. We have significant examples in the treatment of liturgical questions: the liturgical movement was a rediscovery of the *meaning* of things and of their anthropological dimension, a re-creation of a certain liturgical *man*, a restoration of the role of the subject, in reaction to a juridicism that had dried everything

up. The same is true of the way in which the fathers were used, and also the liturgy, as "theological gold-mines". Similarly, the juridical approach to the activity of a council fails to take important human factors into account, or the ethical and religious conditions for reaching the truth. A good example of this, which is almost monstrous, is found in the remark by Joseph de Maistre (1862): "What is the point of an ecumenical council when the pillory will do?"

The fathers, on the other hand, and the ancient tradition, are fully preoccupied with these questions. They see the conciliar decision as realized and guaranteed by God, and as the result of a process, itself guided or inspired by God's grace, whose aim is to restore unity to man who has become fragmented. It is not without significance that the opening of the council is preceded by fasting and carried out in prayer; that, at least according to the present *Ordo concilii celebrandi*, each sitting opens with a celebration on the part of the eucharistic synaxis. The council itself is a celebration—i.e., something quite different from a conference, but something different too from a ceremony or rite. Ancient patristic history conceived the whole of Christian life and the activity of the Church itself (which it considered to be the same thing) as an attempt to re-form within us our likeness to God. whose image, without of course having been totally lost, has been disfigured, dirtied, tarnished, and effaced. It was also described as reassembling man, and reuniting the scattered fragments of Adam.

The reform of the Church, which was traditionally linked to the councils, implied a coming together. It is moving to see Jean Gerson reaffirm this profound relationship in the scarcely uplifting climate of the Council of Constance in 1415:

> The Holy Spirit is the "efficient cause" of the council; its "formal cause" is the gathering together here of the holy fathers; its "final cause" is the glorification of God, and its "material cause" the renewal of all men. [Mansi XXVIII, 537.]

This relationship is even more profound than any anthropological implications of ecclesiology. The examination of man made in God's image must be taken right to its *theo*-logical roots. God is a trinity of persons in a perfect unity of life, of wisdom, of power, and of action *ad extra*. Men can only reproduce his likeness by being persons united in a communion: "That they may be one *as* we are one" (Jn 17:22). It is this idea, already found in the thought and exhortations of St Ignatius of Antioch, that is the inspiration of the famous expressions of Tertullian, which occur even before his adoption of Montanism—in *De baptismo*, for example (A.D. 200–206):

> Where the three are present, Father, Son and Holy Spirit, the Church, which is the body of the three, is also present.

That this is an allusion to the juridical principle "tres faciunt collegium", as is suggested by Hatch and

Mersch, is quite possible, and it may be noted in this connection that canon law has itself adopted this principle (*CIC* 1002), but neither the biblical context nor the theological reference to the Trinity should be forgotten.

The principal biblical texts are those which define: first, the law of the concordant testimony of two or three witnesses; and secondly, the law of prayer in common:

> A single witness shall not prevail against a man for any crime or for any wrong in connection with any offence that he has committed; only on the evidence of two witnesses, or of three witnesses shall a charge be sustained [Dt 19:15.]
>
> Again I say to you, if two of you agree on earth about anything they ask, it will be done for them by my Father in heaven. For where two or three are gathered in my name, there am I in the midst of them. [Mt 18:19–20.]

The principle from Deuteronomy is without doubt primarily juridical; but, on the one hand, it has anthropological overtones, beyond its procedural function, of a humanitarian and fraternal inspiration, and, on the other, it has been so often quoted, and applied to so many situations in the New Testament (cf. Mt 18:16; 1 Cor 13:1; 1 Tim 5:19; Heb 10:28; Jn 8:16f.) that we should see in it a more general meaning, concerning the kind of behaviour that the word of God suggests to us – that by which we may best imitate the manner of existence and action of

God himself: which is the purpose and profound inspiration of ecclesiastical law. It is finally a question of imitating God himself, who has so often given double testimony (cf. Jn 5:31f; 8:13–17; 1 Jn 5:7f.) and, in his works, provided examples of duality in unity: to take a few examples almost at random: man and woman, soul and body, the two sides of the body (i.e., two eyes, two hands, etc.) heaven and earth, sun and moon (*duo luminaria*), two powers, Peter and Paul, Moses and Elijah, the two pillars of the temple, the two cherubim of the ark, etc. The reason for this is, doubtless, that he is himself plurality of persons in unity, agreement of several in one.

These same consideration also form the background of the logion: "If two or three . . ." It is easy to produce Jewish parallels, but harder to prove that they are anterior to the gospel. It is more relevant to our subject to find examples of its resonance in Christian theology. First, in ecclesiology – Tertullian, while still in his earlier line of thinking, wrote that "you should accept that the Church is present even in three people", and of "the Church which the Lord has established in three people". (*PL* 2, 120; 2, 1080.) St Ephraim, copying an agraphon which promised the Lord's presence to the solitary individual, added a gloss to the logion in question:

"When there are three of us" we constitute, as it were, the Church which is the perfect body of Christ and the visible image of him.

At the turn of the eighth and ninth centuries, St Theodore Studites wrote:

> Let us not scandalize the Church of God, which is constituted by three true believers, as is attested by the saints. [*PG* 99, 1049B.]

These are different ways, perhaps a little materialistic and quantitative, of expressing the trinitarian nature of the Church, which is the deep-seated principle of its essential conciliarity. The council, as Dom Gréa says so magnificently, is a sort of concelebration: it imitates the council of the divine persons. A juridical approach neither understands not has sympathy for, a concelebration, at the level of liturgical life. In their treatises *De conciliis*, neither Passaglia nor Palmieri quote Mt 18:20, although this verse is classic on the subject.

Perhaps the greatest difference between ancient patristic ecclesiology and modern ecclesiology is that the former included anthropology, while the latter is merely the theory of a system, a book of public law; one may ask if the system requires men of a certain quality, or if it considers them interchangeable. The anthropology of patristic ecclesiology is that of a human communion, which finds its full authenticity in and through that communion, because in this way it rediscovers a resemblance to God. This is the meeting place of the anthropology and the ecclesiology, and it is this "communicating humanity" which is the subject of the Church's actions and attributes. A tradition exists on this question that should one day be restored and infused with new life.

At the deepest level this tradition is expressed in St Augustine's theology of *unitas*, according to which truth is safeguarded by unity as such; the forgiveness of sins is obtained and the power of the keys is exercised by unity. When St Augustine writes ' [God] established the teaching of the truth in the chair of unity" (*PL* 33, 403) he is not speaking of the see of Rome, as is all too often believed and asserted, but of each and every see, and of their totality, existing in the *unitas*. It is in unity as such that truth is preserved. Here, linked to a supernatural, fully biblical, and Christian anthropology, we have a thesis which a decidedly ecclesiological value, which encompasses the precious part of truth contained in the "Sobornost" of the Eastern orthodox, whose ecclesiological position is above all anthropological. Before the victory of a unilateral juridical theory, dominated by the idea of a pontifical monarchy, Catholic tradition had preserved the idea that the true *subject* of infallibility is the *ecclesia universalis*. The documentary evidence needed to explain this properly would require a special study, which I hope to undertake one day. Suffice it here to call upon Aquinas, "who speaks for the whole School":

The universal Church cannot err, because it is governed by the Holy Spirit, who is the Spirit of truth: this the Lord promised to his disciples, when he said: "When the Spirit of truth comes, he will guide you into all truth" (Jn 16:13). [*ST* II–II, 2. 1, a. 9, sed c.]

. . . the faith of the universal church, which cannot fail, as the Lord said: "I have prayed for you that your faith may not fail" (Lk 22:32). [*ST* II–II, 2.2, a. 6, ad 3.]

If we consider divine providence, which through the Holy Spirit guides its Church against error, as John 16 promised in saying that the Spirit would come and teach all truth—all truth, that is, which concerns those things necessary for salvation—it is at once clear that the judgment of the universal Church cannot err in matters pertaining to the faith. [*Quodl* IX, 16.]

This explains why, traditionally, questions of faith concerning the universal Church, which is the subject of indefectible faith, demanded the calling of a general council a representation of the whole Church. The council, a gathering of the Church in its *totality and unity*, is the realization and expression of the Christian man as a man of communion and, on the episcopal level, what might be called a collegial man. And in his profound theology of the unity of the Church through communion, which he develops when discussing the notion of schism, Cajetan does not forget to add: "The sign of this single whole and its parts is the unity of a universal council". This theology of Cajetan's could be transposed into anthropological terms, in an examination of what it means to be a man of communion. With regard to the unity of the Church, this is a reality which is coextensive with the whole of the Church's existence, and which transcends therefore the transitory and "extraordinary" moment represented by a council. In speaking of councils this essential aspect of things must not be forgotten, as it seems to have been forgotten by the more juridical treatises.

At a more ordinary level of the Church's life tradition expressed itself in a whole system of communalism, of councils and agreements, of which this modern age, steeped in absolutist notions, has no longer any idea. This system was inspired by a conception of man according to which we need the fraternal help of others. Certain biblical texts were often quoted, such as Prov 18:19. Here, for example, is a typical passage from the fifth ecumenical council (the second Council of Constantinople, A.D. 553):

> Nor, in common discussions concerning the faith, can the truth be made clear in any other way, since every man needs the support of his neighbour, as Solomon says in Proverbs: "A brother bringing help to his brother will be exalted like a fortified city" (Prov 18:19). [Mansi IX, 370.]

God intervenes and acts where several are *gathered together*. It was when the apostles were gathered together in prayer that they received the Holy Spirit. Möhler who remarked upon this, cites two phrases dear to the author of Acts: *homothumadon*, and *epi to auto*; the first of these expresses the idea of forming a single body, a true community, and therefore of having a single spirit, of acting "as one man" (cf. Acts 2:46; 5:12; 15:25); while the second, by itself, means "in the same place", but with an overtone of reunion and of being together. (Cf. Acts 1:15; 2:1, 44.) It is always the same idea: the Spirit is given to the unified man, to the fraternal gathering of two of three. In his *Vita S. Remigii*, Hincmar of Rheims illustrates this by recounting a miracle, which is all the more interesting in that the "three" gathered together are the bishop—and the king and queen. This is how "the Lord was pleased to show forth clearly what he promised to all the faithful: Where two or three . . .". (*PL* 125, 1159A.)

2. *The special presence of the Holy Spirit*

Councils are "assembled in the Holy Spirit". This is a classic formula which has almost become a matter of form: (DS 265, 1500, 1501, etc.) *Sancta Synodus in Spiritu Sancto (legitime) congregata* ("the holy council legitimately assembled in the Holy Spirit"), where *legitime* refers to the council's validity or canonicity, and *sancta* evokes the *congregatio* or *ecclesia sanctorum*, i.e., the coming together of men dedicated to the service of the gospel, in continuity with the first Church of "saints" in Jerusalem, and so refers to the council's institution by the Lord. The council is truly assembled, *congregata*. It is assembled by and in the Holy Spirit who, unseen, is the most important person in the gathering—"in the presence of the Holy Spirit and his angels". as the Council of Arles (A.D. 314) has it. (Mansi II,

469.) Sometimes the fathers are said to be assembled in a certain place *with* the Holy Spirit (DS 265), or again *by* the Holy Spirit. (*PL* 54, 1114.) In keeping with the theology of the relations between Christ and his Spirit, however, it is usually an intimate action of "prompting" or "inspiration" that is attributed to the Holy Spirit (Hartel, 655; etc.), while the act of presiding is attributed to Christ (*PG* 77, 293; etc.)—understood mystically, but represented visibly by placing an image of Christ in the middle of the basilica, or more often the book of the gospels open, on a throne.

Christ and the Holy Spirit are not there passively; they bring about the council, in a supreme way; they constitute it as an assembly united in truth. It is true both, on the one hand, as we have already seen, because the Spirit is given to those who are fraternally of one mind, and on the other hand because he creates this unanimity: in the same way that St Augustine distinguishes between the operation by which the Holy Spirit prepares the way for unity or brings man into the body of Christ, and that by which he establishes the link of unity or perfect peace, or acts as the inspiration of the members who share the communion of the body (*PL* 37, 1092)— in the same way that the *initium fidei* is already supernatural, being the seed of faith itself. "The assembly of priests is a witness to the presence of the Holy Spirit", wrote Pope Celestinus 1 to the Council of Ephesus (*PL* 50, 505): the fact of two or three gathering together in Christ's name is a guarantee of the Spirit's presence. There are countless examples to show that the councils felt themselves to be "inspired", that is, to have been visited by the Holy Spirit. These words, or words very like them, are continually to be found: "At the prompting and inspiration of the Holy Spirit . . ." It is Christ and the Holy Spirit who act in the councils and who are the real authors of their decrees, so that the final judgment, that particular act which is strictly speaking the conciliar act, will be the common act of the assembled college *and* of the Holy Spirit. The Lord and the Spirit sometimes even intervene visibly. (Hartel 855.) Thus the conciliar decisions are of God, and made by his authority. Note the way in which the Council of Ephesus worded the condemnation of Nestorius: "Our Lord Jesus Christ, whom he blasphemed, decides, by the holy council, that Nestorius is divested of the episcopal dignity and expelled from the whole body of bishops" (DS 264). In the writings of the fathers, it goes without saying—and not so much by way of juridical affirmation about the authority of bishops, or of the council representing Christ or assuming the authority communicated to them by him, but rather by way of an *actualist* approach—in the writings of the fathers, it is God, Christ, the Holy Spirit, who *act* in the legitimate and holy assembly. As Constantine (or a contemporary of Constantine) wrote after the Council of Nicea:

Three hundred bishops and more affirmed that

there was one single faith, and only one, in conformity with the authentic truths of God's law. . . .
Let us then accept the judgment made by the
Pantocrator. . . . For the judgment of three hundred
bishops is nothing else than the judgment of God,
above all for the reason that the Holy Spirit,
residing in the minds of these great men, has
clearly revealed God's will. There is no longer any
room for doubt. [*PG* 67, 85.]

The councils simply serve as human organs for the
Holy Spirit, to formulate decisions "which the Holy
Spirit has published through their mouths". (Mansi
XII, 82.)

Unanimity is at the same time the fruit and the
sign of this active presence of the Holy Spirit; it is a
sign or criterion for those who observe it. It is his
distinguishing mark, in keeping with his quality as
"spirit" which can, remaining one and the same,
become present and act within each person. "They
were different persons", wrote St Ambrose of the
apostles, "but the carrying out of their work was the
same in all of them, because the Holy Spirit is one
and the same". (*PL* 16, 724.) This unity—or, better,
unicity—of action whose subject is plural, and even a
great numbers of persons, is precisely the conciliar
act as such. This is why the councils and fathers
continually attribute their unanimity, or the agreement and *consensus* which produces the conciliar
decision, to the Holy Spirit. Here are several significant texts:

Now if the apostles say: "It has seemed good to the Holy Spirit and to us" (Acts 15:28), not making themselves co-ordinate with, but subordinate to, the power of the Spirit, inasmuch as they are led by him and speak of their own and the Spirit's knowledge and opinion and even power as if they were one, you on the other hand are trying to bring the Spirit down to the level of the creature. [*PG* 29, 740–41.]

Since indeed all priests of the Lord have, through the guidance of the Holy Spirit, agreed together on one opinion . . . [*PL* 54, 288–9.]

By the inspiration of the Holy Spirit all agreeing together, in accord and harmony the one with the others . . . [Mansi XI, 662.]

With the accord of the most Holy Spirit agreeing and brought together the one with the others . . . in harmony and unanimity, taking their words from the Holy Spirit. . . . [Mansi XIII, 404C.]

The assembly is the place where a special presence of God and of his Spirit is assured.

We may well ask here what *special* sort of presence is meant. The notion of presence is simple enough, but presence is realized in different ways. It can be an immediate datum of knowledge. In reference to God the classic distinctions are between the presence of the immeasurable and the presence of grace, the consummation of which is the presence of glory. But there is also the presence of God and of Christ in sacramental actions (cf. DS 3840); there is Christ's eucharistic presence; there has been, in him, the presence of the hypostatic union. All these supernatural forms of presence, however, have something in common which is an essential feature of any presence of God in his creature, namely, an action by God, a causality. God is everywhere and nowhere. With regard to his creature he is present where he acts. The presence of the hypostatic union and the eucharistic presence only exist by the action of the word assuming a human nature, and that of Christ assuming the offered gifts of bread and wine. The presence of unmeasurability is explained by divine causality, at least in the thomist school. The presence of grace (and that of glory) is a result of the act by which God enables us to have *him*, "sicuti est", as the object of our knowledge and our love, as our partner in an intimate communion. God is truly there where he acts, and the modes of his presence are simply the modes of the relationship between us and him, created in us by his action. God's presence is always royal and sovereign.

What is the presence of God, attributed to the Holy Spirit, proper to a conciliar assembly—a presence whose subject, the beneficiary of a specific action by God, is the assembly or college as such? It is the presence promised to the institution as such by God who calls it into being, and who is faithful to the promise that he made freely. This is how the Lord is present in a sacramental action: in an absolution, in a consecration, in an ordination, in a marriage, celebrated according to the gospel institution as defined in the Church's rites and discipline. The presence of the Lord, by his Spirit, in the councils is of the same sort; not that councils, as such, are of divine institution, for, although conciliarity is essential to the Church, the concrete form of the councils does not belong to the structure which the Lord gave his Church. There is nonetheless a certain structure to which the Lord freely guaranteed his presence by a formal promise:

> All authority in heaven and on each has been given to me. Go therefore and make disciples of all nations . . .; and lo, I am with you always, to the close of the age. [Mt 28:18–20.]
>
> For where two or three are gathered in my name, there am I in the midst of them. [Mt 18:20.]

To be gathered together in his name (*eis onoma*) means to be gathered together for his sake, in order to strengthen our belonging to him. When it refers to prayer it means to pray according to the conditions of his will, and more precisely by realizing the fraternal relationship of communion (Mt 18:19–20), of forgiveness (18:21–35; 5:23–5), that is to say of love, which the Lord makes an element and condition, as it were, of the authenticity of our relationship with him (see Mt 25:31–46). The theological event of the Holy Spirit is conditioned by the anthropological truth according to which we refashion within ourselves the image of God. This is a structure of the covenant which is comparable, in its own way, to those more institutional, even juridical, structures of the covenant: the sacraments or the hierarchical ministries. This is certainly how the fathers understood it; one has but to read Pope Sylvester's letter to the Council of Arles in A.D. 314, or the text of St Basil (Didymus?) already quoted (*PG* 29, 740–41). It will be seen that, according to them, when the conditions are met and the structures of the covenant are respected, namely, mutual love and the fraternal gathering of two or three in his name, then the Lord fulfils his promise, which is effectively linked to these conditions.

His promise is to be there as Lord, i.e., as someone to whom all power in heaven and on earth has been given; therefore the actions of his apostles on earth, in the framework of the covenant and of the mandate they have received, are assured of his "presence", which is dynamic and efficacious. The legitimacy of the council ensures that it is in line with a structure of the covenant to which is attached the promise of this presence—not that the mere juridical and formal legitimacy suffices, but the canonical legitimacy is a first condition that is very holy. The whole of the ancient and medieval Church was of the opinion that God's grace was linked to the observation of canonical rules, as to a sort of sacramental sign. One should doubtless give more place to the freedom of the event of grace, but this gives us a good idea of the specific mode of presence we are dealing with.

It is, I suggest, a *covenantal presence*, by which God has promised to be active, by his grace, in ecclesial actions, when the conditions are met and the structures of the covenant respected. It is therefore the presence linked to the action by which God honours his promise and guarantees his assistance to those actions accomplished within the framework of the covenant. It is an active presence which supposes the presence by which God established the covenant first of all, in electing the Church by grace, and in consecrating it to himself. He established it as a Church by creating these structures of the covenant: faith, sacraments and instituted ministry. To these structures, founded by the incarnate word, and also to the first community assembled according to them, God gave his Spirit, which inhabits and remains in them. He is the love of God inhering in his creation, the Church, and uniting it to God according to the dispositions of the economy of salvation, which find their realization in the incarnation of the Son of God and in the pasch of Christ.

When the members of the Church, and especially those who are ordained as ministers, put the structures of the covenant into operation Christ and his Holy Spirit are present as an internal motivating force. This is the kind of presence which is proper to the conciliar assembly, for the council, without belonging to the essential structure of the Church, eminently fulfils one of the conditions laid down by the Lord himself.